This is a Parragon Book
First published in 2002

Parragon
Queen Street House
4 Queen Street
Bath BA1 1HE, UK

Copyright © Parragon 2002

ISBN: 0-75258-244-5

A copy of the CIP data for this book is available from the British Library upon request.

The right of Clive Somerville to be identified as the author of this work has been asserted in accordance with Section 77 of the Copyright, Designs and Patents Act of 1988.

Editorial, design and layout by Essential Books, 7 Stucley Place, London NW1 8NS

Printed and bound in China

Yahoo! screen shots on pages 66, 137, and 142 are reproduced with permission of Yahoo! Inc. © 2000 by Yahoo! Inc. YAHOO! and the YAHOO! logo are trademarks of Yahoo! Inc.

Screen shot on page 74 is reprinted with permission from CNET, Inc. © Copyright 1995-2001. www.cnet.com

Screen shot on page 134 has been reproduced with permission from Forte Inc. Agent © Forte 1995-2001

The author and publishers have made every reasonable effort to contact all copyright holders. Any errors that may have occurred are inadvertent and anyone who for any reason has not been contacted is invited to write to the publishers so that a full acknowledgement may be made in subsequent editions of this work.

Understanding the Internet

Clive Somerville

Contents

Introduction to the Internet   5

Getting Online   17

The Wonder of the World Wide Web   41

Multimedia: Software, Sound and Vision   71

Shopping Online   97

Understanding E-mail   111

Talk Talk   129

Look After Yourself   147

Super Surfing   169

Glossary   179

INTRODUCTION TO THE INTERNET

If you'd asked most people six or seven years ago what the Internet was, the chances are you'd have been met with a blank look. But unless you've been locked away in the Big Brother house since then, you can't fail to have heard of it – in that short time, it's become as much a household word as 'TV' or 'telephone'. So what exactly is it?

Where does the word come from?

The word 'Internet' is short for 'interconnected networks', which describes it perfectly – millions of computers worldwide, all connected in a completely unstructured way, to allow users to access information on just about anything under the sun. You can think of it in a similar way to a switchboard in an office – you have a network of office phones, which in turn are connected to a national network of phones, which again are linked to a series of telephone networks all over the world. So from your one phone, you can communicate with other phones all over the world. Today, it is estimated that over 300 million people use the Internet, in over 100 countries, and the figure is rising all the time.

How does it work?

The whole system works rather like a giant, global postal system. Each computer, including yours, has a unique address (like that of your house) designated by a number and often a name. When you want to send a message over the Internet, you send it first to a network routing device, known as a gateway. An electronic 'postman' then sends your message from the 'local post office' to the next computer in line, where a second 'postman' moves it on to the next stage and so on until your message reaches its destination.

In the early days of the Internet, these links between computers were provided exclusively by telephone. Now we have added all sorts of other communications, such as cable and satellite, so that the Internet can even be accessed from your TV or mobile phone.

But there's a further problem to solve – how do millions of computers, in over 100 different countries, all using different languages, understand each other over the Internet? The answer is that all the computers speak the same language over the Net. This is called Transmission Control Protocol/Internet Protocol but is more usually known simply by its initials – TCP/IP. Although you may not realize it, you use this format when you set up the Internet connection on your PC – your Internet Service Provider (ISP), the company that provides you with access to the Internet, will be very familiar with the term. Using a 'protocol' (or language) in this way is a bit like a scenario in which people from all over the world have a meeting and decide to use English, for example, to communicate. This saves them having to have their individual language translated into everybody else's languages every time they want to say something, and vice versa. A common language makes communication a lot simpler. It's also helped by the fact that Microsoft has become the dominant company for computer software, and since the 1990s has started to build a lot of Internet features into its programs. This means a large majority of the world's computers are already using a similar language even before they start.

Do I really need to know all this?

It's not vital to know how something works in order to use it, but having an understanding of what happens when you visit the Web or send an e-mail will help you to work out what might have happened if things go wrong, and appreciate just what a wonderful invention it is when things go right! You may have heard some of your friends or colleagues bemoan the slow speed of the Internet at times, or you may have become frustrated at the wait yourself, but when you appreciate the journey that information has to make in order to reach you or your desired destination, you can only marvel at its success rate. Add to that the number of people using the Internet at any one time, and it's a wonder that your message makes it through all that cyber-traffic at all.

Why is the Internet so popular?

The great attraction of the Net is that it means different things to different people. For some, it's a way of catching up with the latest news, for others it's a giant encyclopedia and for yet more people it's a way of keeping in touch by e-mail or making new friends in virtual chatrooms. For many people, the Internet is the World Wide Web, but in fact the Internet refers to the nuts and bolts – the electrical circuitry, if you like – that links all these computer networks together. It is the Internet that allows the Web to operate in the wonderful way that it does. Many hardened PC enthusiasts will tell you that there is almost nothing in your life that you can't organize on the Web – some have even found their perfect partner online. This may seem a bit obsessive to most people, but it does show you just what a major impact the Internet has had on our lives.

Who runs the Net?

No one really, and in a way that's an added attraction. In these times of globalization, multinational companies and centralized government, many see the Net as the last bastion of freedom of expression. Anyone with Internet access and some free web space can set up a website, and anyone with a PC can visit it. Even such powerful database sites as Yahoo! have pretty much given up trying to categorize and index every site on the Web; there are just too many to list, and the number is growing all the time. For many, it's the positive side of globalization – people from all over the world coming together in one big, online community, something that even governments and business tycoons can't control.

Where did it start?

Ironically, for such a symbol of anarchy and freedom of expression, the Internet has its roots in the US military. During the Cold War, the military were looking for a communications system that could withstand a wartime attack. They came up with the idea of having a network connected to other networks, so that if one was put out of action, another could simply take over. The US Defense Agency came up with the Advanced Research Projects Agency Network (ARPANET). To send even small amounts of data from one network to another, the information had to be broken down into more manageable chunks. The idea now known as 'packet switching' was developed to do just that – divide the data into smaller 'packets', each electronically 'labelled' with the address of the computer it was being sent to. It's not hard to see from this how the idea of addresses for e-mail and websites came about.

The idea of an 'Internetwork' gained further support in the 1970s from the scientific community as a means of sharing information amongst their colleagues. In particular, it was the idea of hyperlinks – being able to click on a word or phrase in one document to take you to another related one – that the scientists could see real benefit from: this would allow them to discuss their findings quickly and accurately without having to meet face-to-face. A scientific Internetwork was set up called the Computer Science Research Network (CSNET). There is much dispute as to when this was actually first done, however; the idea of an Internetwork was only really applied to the Internet with the advent of the World Wide Web.

At the end of the 1970s, ARPANET and CSNET combined to form a standard networking system, or 'language', called TCP/IP – the same system that we use today. The dawn of widespread Internet use was promoted by the development of PCs and computer networks in the late 1970s. When the US National Science Foundation agreed to let its network be used by Joe Public in the 1990s, the Internet really took off. Today there are millions of users, and communications technology has enabled the Internet to reach the far outposts of Antarctica, the jungles of South America, and even your grandparents, who swore that they'd never get involved in such new-fangled ideas but then became hooked.

So what can I use the Internet for?

Almost anything you care to mention! The Net can be divided into four main areas:

- **E-mail** – sending electronic mail messages, sometimes with text, image, sound or video files attached, to other users with an e-mail account.
- **The World Wide Web** – what many people think of

as the Internet – the huge and ever-expanding network of websites. There are sites on every subject imaginable. Whether you want to book a holiday to Bangkok, search for a scientific fact about slowworms, listen to a radio station in Russia, or play chess with an opponent from the Czech Republic, it's all here on the Web.

- **Usenet** – Internet newsgroups.
- **File Transfer Protocol (FTP)** – the standard method of transferring files to and from the Internet. It is this system that allows you to download software from websites, upload information to your own website, and even store data on specialized Internet storage sites.

It doesn't look much, does it? But just from these four areas of the Net you'll be able to:

- Send and receive electronic mail to and from other users all over the world, 24 hours a day. And what's more, you don't have to worry about time zones or catching people at a bad time, as they can simply read your message at a time that's convenient for them.

Introduction to the Internet

- Download pictures, music, video and games from the Web to your computer.
- Catch up on the latest news, from constantly updated news sites on the Web.
- Book a holiday, hire a car and find out all about your destination before you go.
- Do your weekly shopping online from a major supermarket, straight to your door. No more battling with endless checkout queues.
- Purchase anything from a CD to a new car online and arrange for delivery direct to your home. If the item you want isn't available in the UK, why not buy it from abroad instead?
- Buy and sell shares with one of the many user-friendly share-dealing sites on the Web.
- Bid for all sorts of items in an online auction – no need to travel the length of the country looking for that elusive curio you've always wanted.
- Use the Web as a giant and constantly updated encyclopedia – forget those bookshelf-bending reference volumes in your living room, just look it up online.

- See what's happening at this very moment almost anywhere in the world, with a webcam site – you can get live pictures straight to your PC from all sorts of locations around the globe, and even view the earth itself from outer space.

- Listen to your favourite radio station online, or find a new one anywhere in the world. With Internet radio you don't have to worry about being in the right place to pick up a good reception.

- Find new friends who share your interests, and discuss them in a newsgroup or chatroom. Or why not play your favourite game with an opponent on the other side of the world?

The Internet may become a major part of your life, either for leisure or work, or it may just be for occasional browsing. But however you use it, there's enough there to satisfy almost every desire you can think of. So have fun, and be warned – it can be very addictive!

One final point. As the computer market is very much PC-oriented, this book assumes you are a PC user. Mac owners access the Internet in broadly the same way, although there are some technical differences.

GETTING
ONLINE

If you follow a few rules, getting connected to the Internet is a relatively simple and inexpensive process. In fact, for such a wonderful resource, it's amazing how easily the home user can tap into it.

To connect to the Internet you need four things:

1. A PC
2. A modem
3. An Internet Service Provider (ISP)
4. A phone line

Choosing a PC

The world of the PC retailer may seem a dark and daunting place, but if you enter it armed with a little forethought and basic know-how, you'll soon be playing the sales assistants at their own game.

Basic or advanced?

The first rule of buying a PC for Internet use is: don't get carried away. Most of us are limited to a certain budget, so it's important to spend the money on the bits you need rather than those you don't. Before you even enter a shop or visit a website, think carefully about what you'll be using your PC for. If you'll be spending most of your time browsing the Web and sending e-mails, together with a bit of letter writing, it may be worth buying a more basic PC, and putting the saving into a bigger monitor. On the other hand, if you want to play games or use graphics programs, you'll need a more advanced model. Many PCs are now sold as fancy packages with items like digital cameras or scanners thrown in. However, if you're not going to use these items, there's little point in having them – and by including them, the retailer may have had to cut corners elsewhere. That said, it's always useful having a printer with your PC, as you're sure to print off web pages at certain times, so try and get a printer thrown in if you can.

Tower or mini-tower?

If you've ever seen PCs in shops, you may have noticed that their rectangular boxes come in two distinct shapes – a horizontal model, often with the monitor on top, and a vertical 'tower' usually situated underneath the desk.

The horizontal box is usually more basic, with the larger tower model either having more advanced features or at least space to add them later. If you think your uses of the PC may grow as you become more familiar with it, choose the tower model. That way, you can add extra items such as more memory, graphics cards, or even different types of connection sockets, later on.

Off the peg or made to measure?

Many PCs are advertised as 'Internet-ready', simply meaning that they are ready to connect to the Internet when you buy them, with access to an ISP provided. These are available for as little as £400, and prices are falling all the time. If you're not sure what to go for, these are often a good bet as they can get you up and running quickly, and are relatively inexpensive – certainly no more pricey than a reasonable stereo system or widescreen TV. Alternatively, you may like to specify certain requirements in your PC, such as processor speed, memory and hard disk capacity, and have it made for you. Don't worry – this is less expensive than it sounds – many retailers already have PCs made up in various combinations and it's simply a matter of deciding which components you'd like in the one you buy.

Processor

The processor, or Central Processing Unit (CPU), is a microchip that acts as the brain of the computer, carrying out millions of calculations a second. The CPU, along with the amount of RAM your PC has (see below) largely determines how fast your computer can operate. The speed of the processor is measured in megahertz (MHz), with 1 MHz meaning it can carry out 1 million power cycles per second – the more cycles a processor can carry out per second, the more calculations it can carry out. Most new PCs have at least a 500 MHz processor, and this is the minimum you should consider. At the other end of the scale, some are now approaching 2 GHz (gigahertz) – a staggering 2 billion cycles per second.

Memory

The Random Access Memory (RAM) of a PC is measured in megabytes (MB) and determines the number of tasks a computer can carry out simultaneously. Most new models normally have at least 64MB, and this is the minimum you should look for. Games and graphics programs eat memory for breakfast, so consider 128MB if you'll be using these.

Screen size

If you're an Internet enthusiast, there's nothing more annoying than having a screen too small to view web pages properly – you're forever scrolling around the page trying to see what that intriguing bit in the corner actually says. Most PCs come with at least a 15-inch monitor, (ask for the viewable size, as part of the screen is tucked behind its casing) but you can choose far bigger screens if you wish. As with televisions, the size of the screen is measured diagonally from one corner to the other. Secondly, if looks and space are important – and, let's face it, the average computer monitor will hardly win any beauty contests – you may like to consider a flat screen 'LCD' (Liquid Crystal Display) or 'TFT' (Thin-Film Transistor) monitor (one without the TV-like protrusion at the back). But beauty comes at a price – these are considerably more expensive than the standard model – although prices are falling all the time.

Watch the warranty

As Murphy's Law says, if something can go wrong, it will – and PCs, even new ones, are no exception. Most new models have at least a one-year warranty against something going wrong and this is the minimum you should accept. Try and get an onsite warranty – whereby the dealer will come to your home to fix it while you wait – rather than having the hassle of having to send it back to the retailer.

The modem

What is a modem?

The word 'modem' is short for Modulator-demodulator, which describes exactly what it does. Phone lines transfer data using analogue signals, but computers use digital data instead. The modem plays the vital role of converting the PC's digital data into analogue signals, to send down your phone line. Another modem at the other end then converts the signal back into digital data, for use with the computer networks that make up the Internet. Similarly, your modem turns any analogue signals it receives back into digital data for your PC to use. In short, it acts as a go-between for your PC and phone line.

Setting the standard

PC development was once a very haphazard affair, with different manufacturers making different types of hardware and software in isolation – and these often failed to understand each other quite spectacularly. One of the main areas this affected was the Internet – not least because computers found it incredibly difficult to communicate with each other when, for example, they were using different types of modems operating at different speeds. To solve this, a standard specification has now been set for modems, and all new modems conform to this standard. Although other specifications still exist, you should look for a modem that conforms to type V.90. This guarantees that the modem will operate at a speed of 56Kbps. See below for a further explanation of modem speed.

The need for speed

The speed of a modem is measured in bits per second (bps). A 'bit' is simply a unit of digital data and the bps refers to the number of these bits that the modem can send down a phone line in one second. Most new PCs now come with a 56K modem, meaning that they can transfer 56,000 bits of data per second, and this is the minimum speed you should buy. In practice, modems never operate at full speed because of blips on the phone line, delays with your ISP or 'traffic jams' on the Internet when lots of people are using it at once. It's also worth remembering that you can't receive data any quicker than it's being sent, so a fast modem won't help you if the problem's at the other end! But in order to use the Internet without too much cursing and tearing your hair out, your 56K modem should run at a speed of at least 33Kbps.

Inside/Outside

Most PCs now come with a built-in modem, which is by far the easiest option. If your computer doesn't have one already, however, you can either buy an internal model (which fits in one of the expansion slots inside the computer tower) or an external one, which you plug into one of the ports at the back of your PC. Although external ones take up precious desk space and look more ungainly than an internal version, they do at least have a series of lights on them to tell you if they're working properly. Meanwhile, if your Internet connection fails with an internal modem, it can be more difficult to discover whether it's the modem playing up or something else. You may also have the option of a PC card modem – an item about the size of a credit card that fits into a corresponding slot on the side of or inside your PC. These were originally invented for laptops, but are being used increasingly in new desktop PCs.

Voice modems

Many modems now come with a built-in speaker and microphone, allowing you to use your PC as a phone. With cheap international calls available over the Internet, this can be a real money-saver. You can even set up your modem to act as an answering machine, with a switch that enables you to swap between voice (analogue) and data (digital) mode. These are hardly essential features, but can be useful optional extras.

Cable modems

Until recently, the only connection available was through the trusty old telephone line. But two or three cable companies are now trying to speed things up for us. Instead of using a conventional telephone line, data is sent down a fibre optic cable – in the same way cable TV is received – and converted by a cable modem installed in your house. For around £25 a month, cable gives you permanent, unmetered Internet access at ten times the speed of a normal phone line. As the connection is always on, there's no frustrating wait to connect to or disconnect from the Internet either – you just click your desktop Internet icon and you're off. What's more, it can handle your phone line at the same time, so you can use the phone even when you're online. It's a bit more expensive than using a standard telephone line, and requires a cable modem to be installed in your home, but it's vastly more convenient. The final chapter in this book, 'Super Surfing', tells you more about such services.

WinModems are losers

You may also come across an unusual type of modem called a WinModem. If so, pretend you didn't. Unlike conventional hardware modems, this type is software-driven and works off your Windows operating system – hence the name. Because the operating system now has to handle another complex piece of equipment, it slows your PC down, and can also be much harder to fix if it goes wrong. You'll probably experience delays on the Internet from time to time with a normal modem, without making things even slower with one of these.

Choosing an Internet Service Provider (ISP)

Choosing the right ISP can get you off to a flying start on your journey along the information superhighway.

What is an Internet Service Provider?

As its name suggests, an ISP, as it's more commonly known, is the company that provides you with access to the

Internet, in the same way, for example, that, if you're in the UK, British Telecom may provide you with access to a line for your telephone. Many companies, of course, are able to provide you with both your phone and Internet access.

What to look for in an ISP

Free Internet access

These days, it's easy to find ISPs providing free access to the Internet. But don't confuse free access with free calls. Access simply refers to the process of connecting you to the Net, but once connected, there's still the cost of the call, just as there would be for a normal phone call.

An affordable helpline

It's all very well offering free Internet access, but if you charge the earth for a helpline, or don't provide one, it's not very helpful at all. Some ISPs will charge as much as 50p or even a £1 a minute, whereas others simply charge the price of a local phone call, or even provide help free. It's not difficult to get connected to the Internet, but newcomers are likely to need a bit of help, so the cheaper that help is, the better. It's also important to have help when you need it – the best ISPs offer support 24 hours a day.

Reliable service

It's surprising how many companies supposedly providing an Internet service provide very little service at all. There's nothing more frustrating than frequently losing your connection, or waiting an age for a web page to display, simply because your ISP cannot cope with demand. There is an argument that ISPs that charge for Internet access are more reliable, but frankly it's perfectly possible for the home PC user to find one that's reliable and free. Obviously, you can't get an accurate idea of reliability until you've tried it, so ask around family and friends for their recommendations and check out the regular surveys of ISPs in PC magazines.

Unmetered calls

It's been a long time coming, but ISPs are now offering a range of fixed-cost call options, rather than pay-as-you-go. Companies such as BT and AOL offer unmetered Internet calls for a fixed monthly fee, so you don't have to watch the clock while you surf. If you use the Internet frequently, and don't want the worry of wondering how big your next phone bill will be, unmetered options can be a great idea. For the best value, look for a deal that includes unmetered use for the time you're online most – obviously the more unmetered time you want, the higher the monthly fee is likely to be – typically between £10 and £25 a month.

Multiple e-mail addresses

Most ISPs now give you several e-mail addresses, which you can use as you like. For example, you can give one e-mail address to each member of your family, or, if you work from home, keep one for business mail and one for personal mail. If you're a gaming enthusiast, you can play games like chess via e-mail and use a separate address for this, as such games can generate a lot of e-mails.

Free web space

Look for an ISP that offers free web space – you can use this to display your own website or store large files like digital photo albums online. Most offer around 25MB of free space, and some are unlimited.

ISP or IAP?

Some ISPs, such as AOL, Freeserve and Zoom, offer their own content, such as news and shopping, as well as the Internet access. It's a bit like having a service provider and a specialized website all in one. Technically, it is these that are called Internet Service Providers while access-only companies are termed Internet Access Providers (IAPs). But as so many providers now offer additional content anyway, the ISP term has become synonymous with both. And just because you choose a particular ISP doesn't mean you have to use their site for your home page – you can change it to any web page you like. You can learn how to do this in the chapter 'The Wonder of the World Wide Web'.

Choosing an ISP that's right for you can sometimes be a process of trial and error and there's no reason why you can't have several ISPs on the go at once. After trying out different ISPs you'll get a better idea of which you like best. Many ISPs offer free trials, too, so you can see what you're getting before you sign up.

Your phone line

Most people in the UK and US already have a phone line installed. The only question is whether you want to tie up your existing phone line with the Internet (meaning you can't make or receive phone calls when you're online) or would rather install a second phone line just for Internet use. Most people prefer the second option, purely for convenience, but of course you're then paying more line rental. A further option is to go for a cable Internet connection (using the same technology that brings you cable TV) as this keeps your phone and Internet connection separate. See the chapter 'Super Surfing' for more details on this.

Connecting up

If you're feeling a bit nervous about getting that little box on your desk to connect up to a huge network of worldwide computers that you can't even see, then fear not. PC manufacturers, ISPs and Microsoft have combined forces in recent years to make getting connected child's play. If you've managed to hook all the bits and pieces of your PC together and are now looking at a bright screen with lots of icons, then you'll certainly be able to manage the next step of connecting it to the Net. All new PCs come with everything you need to get connected pre-installed. It really is just a few clicks away.

There are two ways to connect to the Net, once you've chosen an ISP. You can either:

a) Double-click the snazzy icon on your desktop called Internet Connection Wizard and follow the onscreen instructions, or . . .

b) Insert the CD that your chosen ISP has sent you, (or on many new PCs simply click the icon – marked Freeserve, AOL, Virgin or whatever – that appears on your desktop when you set up your PC) and follow the step-by-step instructions. If you haven't got either of these, contact your chosen ISP and ask them to send you their CD.

Either method does the same thing, but many newcomers find the second method slightly easier, as ISPs, being sensitive to the needs of new customers, set up your Internet software with their own access details, saving you the hassle of working out what information goes where.

So what's on the disk/up the wizard's sleeve?

When you insert your ISP's CD or click on the Internet Connection Wizard, you are configuring the Internet access software that comes with your PC. This is the software that sets up and regulates your PC's connection to the Internet. As you can guess, the most essential part of the process is telling your PC which telephone number to dial up, to give you access to the Internet.

DUN and dusted

New PCs are pre-installed with Microsoft's Dial-up Networking software (DUN), which you then configure with your ISP's access details. If you get stuck at any point, simply contact your ISP for assistance – a helpline number, should be supplied with your CD. By the way, don't confuse Internet access software with Internet application software (the software that allows you to navigate the Web – a web browser such as Internet Explorer, for example). We'll look at application software in the chapter 'The Wonder of the World Wide Web'.

Troubleshooting those connection problems

Even after you've set up your connection, and it's been running fine for days, you may hit the occasional problem. While you're gnashing your teeth in anguish, you can at least remind yourself that it's often due to circumstances at the other end, rather than any incompetence on your part. Small comfort perhaps, but better than nothing in such trying times.

Here are some of the most common problems – which your PC will politely inform you about with an annoying (but nevertheless useful) pop-up window:

1. Your modem cannot detect a dial tone

It sounds embarrassingly simple, but this could be down to your telephone cable not being plugged into the wall correctly – so make sure it's pushed in properly. More seriously, it could be a fault on your telephone line. Simply plug your phone back into the wall and check for a dial tone. If you can't hear one, it's time to get your telephone line seen to.

2. Your PC cannot detect your modem

Remember that the modem is the item that links your PC with the telephone line, so if it's not working properly, you won't get anywhere. As we saw in 'Getting Online', internal modems can be harder to check for faults, and it may be a case of getting your PC tested if all else fails. External modems, on the other hand, have a series of lights to show you that they're working OK. You can also check that an external modem is switched on, and is connected to the correct port (socket) at the back of your PC. Many PCs have a telephone symbol next to the port intended for the modem, or if you're using a USB (Universal Serial Bus) model, any USB port will do. If all your connections are fine, it may be that the software that 'drives' (operates) the modem hasn't installed correctly, so if all else fails, hunt out the software disk that came with your modem, and reinstall the software. It's tiresome but sometimes that's the only way to fix it.

3. TCP/IP problems

As we saw in the first chapter, the Internet works by assigning every computer a unique address, called an

Internet Protocol (IP) address. This is usually a series of numbers, and allows information being sent over the Web to reach its correct destination. However, if your Transfer Control Protocol/Internet Protocol (TCP/IP) settings are incorrect you won't be able to communicate properly with the rest of the Internet. Contact your ISP to make sure you've entered the settings correctly when you set up your Internet connection. Once you've typed in the correct TCP/IP settings, make a note of them on a piece of paper and store it away safely, in case you need to use them again in the future.

4. Password/Username not recognized

When you set up your Internet connection, you are asked for your username (usually assigned to you by your ISP) and a password of your choice. Be careful to type these exactly as you typed them in originally (including upper- or lower-case letters) or they won't be recognized. Many people mistype their password first time round, and then tick the box that says 'Save password'. This means that an incorrect password is being remembered, thus making a connection impossible. If the 'Dial-Up

Networking' pop-up window doesn't appear automatically, go to it by clicking My Computer on your desktop, then selecting Control Panels, then Dial-Up Networking. Now click the icon of your desired connection. The 'Connect to' box appears, showing you details of your username and password. Simply re–type these if they're incorrect, then try connecting again.

5. Engaged tone

Strange as it might sound, you'll sometimes hear the engaged tone, just as you would when using a telephone. This can happen at busy times of the day, when there are too many people trying to dial up the same connection as you. A good ISP should have enough capacity to cope with demand, but not all do. If you get the engaged tone, you'll just have to 'hang up' (disconnect) and try again in a few minutes – just like using the phone!

These are probably the five most common connection problems you can experience, but hopefully they won't be so common that they put you off using the Internet for good. Don't be afraid to use your ISP's helpline either –

once you've checked all the simple things like your telephone connection and so on, contact your ISP for further assistance. They'll be able to take you through the problem step by step and hopefully find a solution. And don't forget that the problem could lie at their end, rather than anything you have or haven't done at your end, so it's worth asking this before you waste hours trying to fix a problem beyond your control.

THE

WONDER

OF THE

WORLD WIDE WEB

What is the Web?

The World Wide Web (WWW, or just 'Web' for short) is an unstructured, global network of resources often containing clickable links that allow you to jump from one document to another. You'll find that most people use the words 'Internet' and 'Web' interchangeably, but in fact there's an important distinction. The Internet refers to the communications network – the powerful server computers, cabling, telephone lines and so on – that links the computer network together. The World Wide Web is one type of visual interface that you can access via the Internet. In the same way, the Windows system on your PC, which provides all the menus, windows and icons on your desktop, is the visual interface of all the bits and pieces that go to make up your computer.

Where did it come from?

We saw in the opening chapter how the idea of an interconnected network of computers (the Internet) was born from military and scientific needs. The scientific community took this idea one stage further to develop the best-known part of the Internet – the Web.

Necessity, we are told, is the mother of invention. The Web as we know it began in March 1989 when Tim Berners Lee, at the CERN scientific institute, became fed up with the mountains of papers on his desk that he was forever having to circulate to colleagues by post or hand. He came up with the idea of connecting all these documents by computer, and inserting links in each one, so that the reader could jump from one document to another. Like all the best ideas, it was brilliantly simple – and it took off in a way he could never have imagined. The term 'World Wide Web' was coined the following year and in 1993 CERN generously declared the Web officially open to all. In the same year, Mosaic – the world's first graphical web browser – was produced by Marc Andreessen. Now the three pieces of the jigsaw were in place – a global network of documents linked together (the Web), made easily viewable with a graphical web browser, and run by the Internet.

Navigating the Web

Assuming you've mastered the mechanics of getting online (see previous chapter), it helps if you can find your way around when you get there. The wonder of the Web – the mind-boggling amount of information it holds – can also be its drawback. Unless you know how to use it, you can soon end up searching for a very small needle in a global haystack. Here are your navigation tools:

1. The web browser

What is a web browser?

Without a web browser you won't get anywhere on the Web – so it's just as well they come as standard on most new PCs. A browser is a software program that allows you to view pages from the Web on your computer screen. The most popular web browsers are Internet Explorer and Netscape Navigator.

What does it do?

When you connect to the Web, the job of the browser is

firstly to display all the elements of your chosen web page as accurately as possible on your screen. Early web pages were text-based, but with the march of technology have come ever more intricate websites, including animated graphics, sound and video clips. Today, it seems web designers are searching for ever more sophisticated ways of attracting your attention to their site.

Once the page has been successfully displayed in the window of your web browser, you can use the various features or 'tools' that come with it to navigate your way around the page, move back and forth between pages on the same site, or move to a different site. The most frequently used tools are displayed on the web toolbar, in your browser window, for easy access. These include:

The URL (address) bar

This is the narrow white rectangular box near the top of the browser window, into which you type the address of the website you wish to visit. In Web-speak, the address is called a URL (Uniform or – Universal – Resource Locator), but users know what you mean by 'website address'. Then press Return and the browser will 'fetch' (download) and display the web page in your browser window. Websites have unique addresses, so it's important to type them carefully – even one dot or letter mistyped means the website may not be found by your browser. When you want to go to a different website, simply type in the new address, press Return and away you go.

Note that other addresses may be typed into this bar too, for example the address of an FTP server (File Transfer Protocol – see the next chapter, 'Multimedia: Software, Sound and Vision').

Back and Forward

The two arrows pointing left and right, like indicators on a car's dashboard, allow you to move back and forth between web pages, just as if you were reading a book. This saves you having to type in the address of the web page in the address bar each time. They make use of the fact that your browser can 'remember' or store the pages you have already visited and simply return to them when you wish.

Stop

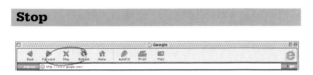

As its name suggests, clicking the Stop button halts the browser trying to download a web page. At busy times, the Internet can churn over interminably slowly and leave you wondering whether waiting for Christmas might be quicker. But if you simply visit another site without stopping the previous one, your browser will continue trying to download it, further slowing down the process.

Refresh (Reload)

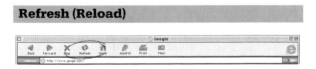

Instead of stopping the download of a web page altogether, you may just want to have another go.

Sometimes, the Web is up to speed, but the page you want doesn't download properly. Clicking the Refresh button begins the download from the start. It's also useful to reload the page if it's one that gets updated frequently, and you want to be sure of having the latest update – for example, the price of an item on an online auction, or an up-to-the-minute view from a webcam at a safari park. Some such sites refresh automatically, but if nothing happens for a few minutes then click the Refresh button to do it manually.

Home

This button takes you back to the page that first displays when you visit the Web each time. Your ISP will have its own default home page, but you can change it to one of your choice. In Internet Explorer, for example, go to Tools, select Internet Options and type the URL of the site you'd like as your home page. Now each time you click the Home button, you'll return to your chosen site.

Search

Your ISP or computer seller will have set up your web browser with its own dedicated search engine(s) – such as MSN, Lycos and Yahoo! – to find websites containing information you are looking for. Clicking the Search button brings up this search facility. Simply type a keyword or phrase into the search box, press Return on your keyboard (or click 'Go' next to the search box) and the browser will search for relevant websites.

Search engines will be covered in greater detail later in this chapter.

Favorites

If you find yourself visiting the same sites frequently, or might like to return to one in the future and won't

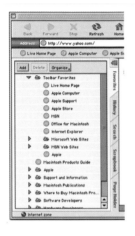

remember the address, you can save them in a list called 'Favorites' in Internet Explorer and 'Bookmarks' in Netscape Navigator. If you wish, you can further organize this list into subfolders, which you can label according to area of interest, e.g. 'Shopping', 'Sport', 'Travel' etc. To make a web page a favourite, simply click on the Favorites button and select 'Add to Favorites'. To visit an existing favourite, click the Favorites button and select the relevant web address from the drop-down list. The browser will then locate the site automatically.

History

This is a list of all the sites you have visited recently. So if you can't remember the address of that site you visited earlier, and you forgot to add it to your Favorites, have a

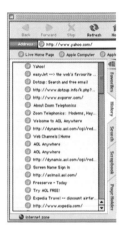

look in the History list instead. You can set the number of days you wish your browser to record these sites, with 'zero' meaning only sites visited that day will be noted.

Print

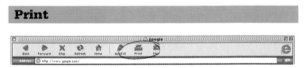

Does exactly what it says – click the button to print out the current web page.

E-mail

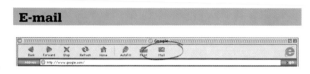

Click this button to open your e-mail program, such as Outlook Express. Similarly, a menu or button in your e-mail program is usually provided to take you straight to the Web. You can learn more about e-mail in the chapter 'Understanding E-mail'.

Don't forget there are also your browser's menus, situated above the toolbar, but understanding the tools above will equip you for your first foray into cyberspace.

2. The URL (Web address)

Why call a spade a spade when you can call it something more confusing? This seems to be the attitude of the person who came up with the term Uniform (or Universal) Resource Locator. What they meant, of course, was the address of the website you want to visit – just as a house address is needed to deliver mail by hand. At first glance, a website address is made up of a confusing mixture of words, abbreviations and dots, but when you break it down, it's easy to understand.

Let's have a look at http://www.microsoft.com, the address of the Microsoft website.

http://

This is called the protocol prefix. It tells your browser where the document is, and what type of protocol or 'language' to use to download it to your screen. HTTP ('hypertext transfer protocol', if you must know!) tells your browser the document it's trying to access is on the Web. Other prefixes include **ftp://** (meaning the document is stored on a File Transfer Protocol server – see 'Multimedia: Software, Sound and Vision') and **news://** (for data stored in a newsgroup such as Usenet – see the chapter 'Talk Talk'). You don't need to type in http:// when entering a web address – your browser enters it automatically.

www.

This is perhaps the part of the web address that people are most familiar with – no prizes for guessing that it stands for World Wide Web. It was originally used to distinguish Web content from other Internet content in the early days of cyberspace, but is no longer strictly necessary. Most web addresses still use it, but it could be any word at all – website owners simply use www. by convention.

microsoft

The domain name. This uniquely identifies the site, and usually includes the name of the company or organization concerned – in this case, Microsoft. The domain name is considered so important in identifying and branding your company on the Net, that some companies have paid hundreds and thousands of pounds to buy a domain name from a previous owner. Some enterprising individuals even registered lots of famous names when the Web first took off, in the hope of selling them to the companies or celebrities concerned for a profit. However, after several court cases, this is now less easy to do and has become known as 'cybersquatting'. In most cases the court ruled that individuals had no right to hoard domain names, and ordered them to give them up. As recently as October 2001, the US stock exchange site NASDAQ won a case against cybersquatters. Domain names are also used in e-mail addresses, as we'll see in 'Understanding E-mail'.

.com

The domain suffix. Technically still part of the domain name, the suffix tells you what type of website it is. The .com suffix suggests it's a commercial site, often in the US, (as Microsoft is), a .co.uk suffix suggests a UK company and .de suggests a German one (Deutschland). Similarly, .edu suggests an educational site, .gov a government site and .org a non-governmental organization. In fact, there are no rules stopping any European company using .com (many do) – so don't assume automatically that you can tell the origin of a website from its domain suffix. Online companies have become so strongly associated with the .com suffix (whether or not they actually use it) that they've even become known as 'dot coms'.

3. Search engines

The third weapon in your armoury for exploring the Web is the search engine. With over a billion pages of text

The home page of the Google search engine

already on the Web and around a million being added every day, it would be almost impossible to find what you're looking for without a helping hand.

What is a search engine and how does it work?

A search engine is a website containing a database of references to other websites. When a website creator adds their site to a search engine, they include hidden 'meta tags' on each page. These are keywords or phrases that describe what their site contains. When you type in a search word or phrase, the engine searches its database, with software called a spider, or metacrawler, for any meta tags matching your terms, and displays a list of possible sites for you to look at. Popular search engines include:

Google (www.google.com)
HotBot (www.hotbot.com)
Yahoo! (www.yahoo.com)
AltaVista (www.altavista.com)
Excite (www.excite.com)
Lycos (www.lycos.com)
Ask Jeeves (www.ask.com)
Go To (www.goto.com)
Looksmart (www.looksmart.com)
MSN (www.msn.com)

Google and HotBot have become increasingly popular because of their user-friendly layout, speedy search method and accurate results, but you'll find all the above a real boost in finding what you want.

Different strokes for different folks

Don't forget you can use more than one search engine – if one doesn't give you the right answers, try another. Bear in mind while you're doing this, however, that the effectiveness of a search engine is only as good as its database and spider software. Many engines use the same search facilities anyway. For example, Go To and HotBot share the same spider. According to Berkeley Library at the University of California, only 40 per cent of a search engine's content is original – the rest will be the same as other engines. For this reason alone, it's worth using more than one search engine to try and hit that original 40 per cent each time.

Using a variety of engines is also important because results depend not just on what you want to search for but how you wish to search for it. There are three ways you can phrase your search, and each engine employs at least one of these methods:

1. Keyword search

Most precise method, especially when combined with Boolean operators.

The most common way of searching, whereby the user types in a keyword or phrase about the subject they are looking for. This is the original search technique and most, if not all engines can use it. (See later in this chapter for further explanation of Boolean operators.)

2. Natural language search

Most user-friendly method, especially for novices, but not as precise as keywords.

Natural language is an idea that is becoming increasingly popular on the Web, and attempts to add a more human touch to surfing. Instead of thinking of a keyword or phrase, you can simply type in your query as a normal question – for example, 'What was Laurel and Hardy's first film?' The search engine will then produce a list of results, in the order it thinks is most relevant. It's ideal for the first-time surfer, but it's not as precise as a keyword search, tending to produce more, but less relevant, results.

Probably the best-known natural language search engine is Ask Jeeves (www.ask.com) and others include AltaVista (www.altavista.com) and a relative newcomer called Northern Light (www.northernlight.com).

3. Concept-based search
Best chance of hitting the jackpot by searching for similar words.

This means the search engine will look for words with a similar meaning to the ones you have requested, giving you a better chance of finding what you want. For example, if you typed in 'cow' the engine would suggest also looking for words like 'bovine' and 'cattle'. Two engines that have this facility are AltaVista and Infoseek (www.infoseek.com).

Searching the search engines

If you want to carry out a wider search, websites called search agents actually search through the search engines. Perhaps the best known of these is Metacrawler (www.metacrawler.com). Rather than searching each engine in turn, a search agent will provide you with results from hundreds of engines at once. Other well-known agents include Copernic (www.copernic.com) and the straightforwardly entitled Search (www.search.com).

What's new?

To keep pace with the latest search-engine developments, it's worth paying a visit to the Search Engine Watch site (www.searchenginewatch.com). This site shows how various search engines are updating their technology, so that you can locate the fastest and most effective engine for your specific needs. Another comparison site is the rather dramatically entitled Search Engine Showdown (www.searchengineshowdown.com), allowing you to see how different search engines perform against each other.

Portals

An excellent way of accessing useful information all in one place is to use a portal. These are websites that contain not only search engines, but also their own specialized content, and additional services such as e-mail, chatrooms (see 'Talk Talk') and a shopping directory. If you've not been on the Web before, they give you a pretty good overview of what's out there. You can often customize the content of a portal to your own needs – the portal in question will show you how to do this. Perhaps the only criticism of portals is that their search engines are not always the best, and you may therefore be better off using a specialized engine to find what you want. Well-known portals include Yahoo! (www.yahoo.com), Excite (www.excite.com) and AOL (www.aol.com), which is also an ISP. Although the primary aim of such portals is self-promotion to make money, the user often benefits from the high-quality services that result from this: it's a very competitive market and portals want you to visit their site rather than anyone else's. Many will encourage you to make their site your home page, and this isn't a bad idea – let's face it, navigating the Web can be rather confusing, and a portal can provide easy, organized access to all sorts of exciting web content.

And your specialized subject is . . .

If you have a specialized interest or subject, try using a subject directory. These search for websites on a particular subject, and often pick up sites that more generalized search engines miss. A good place to start is the Directory Guide (www.directoryguide.com), which contains lists of hundreds of directories, arranged by subject. Another nice touch is that, unlike ordinary search engines that are complied by a spider, directories are compiled by real people with an interest in that subject. It adds a comforting human element to the automated world of the Web.

What's the Word?

One of the biggest complaints from surfers is that, even when using a search engine, they are given hundreds of irrelevant results and still have to sift through these to find what they want. The solution is to be more precise with your search phrases. The more exact you can be about the type of sites you're looking for, the more a search engine can narrow down its search and produce relevant results. For example, if you type in the word 'football', you may get results for Association football, rugby football and American football, whereas if you use the word 'soccer' you are only referring to the first of these. It's also a good idea to use Boolean operators, as described below.

Boolean operators

Named after the English mathematician George Boole, these are words such as AND, OR and NOT that create relationships between the various words in your search phrase. Many engines use the plus (+) and minus (-) signs for AND and NOT respectively. The + sign usually means 'must have this word'; the - sign usually means 'must not have this word'. Experiment with different engines (some will even tell you which Boolean operators they recognize) until you work out the most effective method. For some reason (probably because they seem unimportant within the phrase), most search engines ignore Boolean operators if they are in lower case, so always write them in capital letters. If you type in a phrase without Boolean operators, such as Laurel Hardy, the search engine usually assumes you mean Laurel OR Hardy, so be careful what you type: you may have meant Laurel AND Hardy (sites that contain both words) or Laurel NOT Hardy (sites that contain just Laurel but not Hardy). You can also combine Boolean operators, to narrow down your search still further – a technique known as 'nesting'. For example, if you don't want any information about Laurel and Hardy's classic film *Way Out West*, you could type in Laurel AND Hardy AND (NOT (Way Out West)). But be warned – because of the different Boolean operators search engines use, this won't work on every engine. Although not strictly a Boolean operator, the use of quotation marks round your key phrase can also help. If you just type in Oliver Hardy, for example, the search engine is likely to look for sites that contain both, or either of these words. Therefore you could end up with a lot of irrelevant results about other people called Oliver (or Hardy). Putting quotation marks round the phrase, as in 'Oliver Hardy', ensures the engine treats your words as one phrase and looks for sites containing the whole name.

Don't know much about history . . .

Don't forget that handy History button on your web browser toolbar, too. If your PC crashes while you're looking at your search results and you want to find them again, simply click the History button and select the page of results from the list.

Get help!

Just like the programs on your PC, search engines have their own Help section, giving handy tips on how to use their search tools, and information about what search services they offer. If you're unsure how to use a search engine, the Help section can be a great place to start.

A help page from the popular search engine Yahoo!

Parlez-vous français?

Because of the global nature of the Web, search engines often throw up foreign-language sites. You could have hit on a really useful site but unless you're a talented linguist, it will all seem double Dutch. One helpful solution is to employ the free services of the Babel Fish at www.babelfish.altavista.com on AltaVista's site. Named after the talented translating sea creature from the Hitch Hiker's Guide to the Galaxy novels, using it couldn't be simpler. Click on the button marked Website next to the translation box on the Babel Fish home page. Type in the address of the website you wish to translate, in the narrow white box provided. Select the languages you are translating to and from (e.g French into English). Then, click the Translate button. Hey presto! It's now in English.

Here is the news

An excellent way of going straight to the latest news story or share prices is to use a website with a 'ticker' – a stream of information that runs across the top of your screen. When a headline or story catches your eye, simply click on it and you'll be taken to the page for the full story. Then simply return to the ticker when you've finished. The BBC (www.bbc.co.uk) has a continually updated ticker facility for all the latest news. Other sites provide a 'mini window' that sits at the top of your screen, updating regularly. One of the best examples of this is the Cricinfo site (www.cricinfo.com), which offers an updated scorecard of cricket matches in progress. These facilities used to be called 'channels' by Microsoft, but the last operating system that used the term was Windows 98 – it doesn't appear in Windows Me or Windows XP. The only drawback to using such a feature is that you have to be online the whole time, which can get expensive with a pay-as-you-go connection, though it's fine if you use a fixed-price service.

If all else fails . . .

If you can't find what you want by any other method, it's always worth making an educated guess at the full web address. As we saw earlier, companies (and individuals) view their domain name as a very important part of their online identity, and so will often try to use one that is as close to their name as they can. If you're attempting to find the site of a company or celebrity, for example, try www.companyname.com and www.celebrityname.com. You'll be surprised what you can turn up.

Handy Hints for Web Navigation

1. **Get to know your web browser.** The chances are you'll be using either Internet Explorer or Netscape Navigator, so experiment with the tools on offer, and consult the onscreen Help menu. You'll also find websites offering further advice.

2. **Bookmark useful sites.** It's a lot easier selecting a previously visited site from a Favorites list than trying to remember the web address or searching the Web all over again. Don't forget to organize your bookmarks into folders of categories too.

3. **Use the help on offer.** Instead of staring blankly at a search engine or portal, look for the Help section to guide you through the procedure.

4. **Ask yourself a simple question when looking for information:** how would I find this if I didn't have the Web? This will help you focus your search before you start, and enable you to make better use of search facilities.

5. **Type with care.** It's very frustrating to keep getting messages saying 'No results match your search' when you've typed in 'Laurer and Harde' instead of

'Laurel and Hardy'. Remember that minor words typed in capital letters will often get more attention than lower-case ones. If you know the address of a website, make sure you type it correctly – one letter or full stop out of place and your browser may not find the site.

6. **Use Boolean operators to create relationships between your keywords.** This tells the search engine whether you want to exclude certain associated words from your search.

7. **Enjoy the experience.** Even if it takes a while to track down the information you want, it's still a lot quicker than going all the way to a library and hunting it out by hand. Although we haven't quite put the whole world on the Web yet, it's still the largest information resource available on the planet. It's a wonderfully exciting place to be, so try and enjoy the journey, rather than becoming frustrated with the delay at getting there.

MULTIMEDIA:

SOFTWARE,

SOUND

AND

VISION

The beauty of the Web is that it's not just for looking at – it's also a giant supply store for your PC. There are all manner of tantalizing titbits up for grabs – much of it completely free. Some of the most exciting areas of the Web contain multimedia content – a mixture of text, pictures, sound and video. Apart from general reference information, there is an astounding range of games, music and videos, often downloadable in a matter of minutes. And you can also grab a free media player to play multimedia files – if you haven't got one on your PC already.

What is a download?

The word 'download' simply means to transfer a file from another computer on the Internet to your PC – for example to obtain a file from the Web. Remember that download only refers to a transfer going to your computer – if you send a file from your PC to another computer on the Internet, this is called an upload. If you think of the Internet being a fluffy cloud floating above you, you'll easily remember which way is up and which way down.

A download status window

How do I download files?

Computer technology has made this a remarkably easy process. Websites endeavour to make finding and downloading material as easy as possible – so you'll return to their site frequently. Very often it's just a matter of clicking on an icon or text hyperlink that says something like 'click here to download'. The file download window appears on your screen and asks you whether you want to open the file from its current location (i.e. another computer connected to the Web) or save it to disk (download it), so click the second option then click OK. As the download begins, a download status window appears, showing the download in progress. A bar at the bottom of the window slowly fills with blue, and when it is completely coloured in, the download is complete. If you're downloading an image, sound or music file, you can usually play this straight from your desktop by double-clicking on the downloaded file, but if you're downloading software (such as a plug-in) you'll need to follow the onscreen guide to install it onto your system.

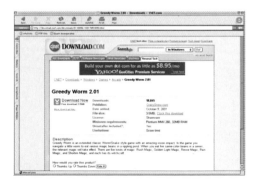

Download.com offers free or very cheap software online

Where can I download software from?

Some websites are dedicated to providing all sorts of software that you can download for free (freeware), for a small 'honesty payment' after downloading it (shareware) or as pay-before-you-download software. There is some great free or very cheap software available, so take full advantage of these very handy sites:

Download (www.download.com)
Shareware (www.shareware.com)
File Farm (www.filefarm.com)
Tucows (www.tucows.com)
WinFiles (www.winfiles.com)

How long will it take?

How long is a piece of string? The download time depends on (a) the size of the file you're downloading and (b) the transfer rate – the speed at which your modem can transfer the data down your phone line to your PC. To get a rough estimate, divide the file size by the transfer rate, which is shown in the status window. For example, if the File size is 500KB and the transfer rate is 5Kbps, it will take about 100 seconds. The status window usually gives the estimated time left for downloading, but this is not always very accurate.

What can I do if it's taking ages?

There are four ways to speed things up:

1. Use a download accelerator program such as Download Accelerator (www.downloadaccelerator.com), which can make downloads up to three times as fast for certain kinds of files.

2. Alternatively, consider a download scheduler program. These arrange your downloads for less busy times on the Internet, and can even resume an interrupted download later on if you wish. A couple of good schedulers are RealDownload (www.real.com) and Go!Zilla (www.gozilla.com).

3. Look for a compressed version of the file you want to download too – many are compressed by software such as WinZip (shown by a .zip file suffix), making the file size much smaller before you start. You'll need to 'unzip' it when it arrives at your end, so it's worth downloading and installing the WinZip program from www.winzip.com before you start.

4. Finally, try and choose downloads from sites that use FTP (File Transfer Protocol). This is one of the original ways of transferring files, and it's still one of the fastest. Some download schedulers/accelerators will look automatically for FTP sites.

Be prepared

Most downloads will go straight into your Documents folder by default, or one marked Downloads. As you collect more items, you may wish to organize them in a folder system of your own, so you can find them quickly.

Play it with a plug-in

Before you get carried away downloading music and video, it's a good idea to have something to play them on – in the same way that it's not a very bright idea to buy CDs if you haven't got a hi-fi! The software you need to play your multimedia files is called a plug-in and there are various models around. A plug-in is simply a program that adds on to a larger program to give it more functions. Some multimedia plug-ins have been branded 'media players', and are often included in your browser. For example, Internet Explorer has Windows Media Player already built in, and Netscape has WinAmp. The other big names in this area are RealPlayer (which is available at www.real.com) and QuickTime, made by Apple (www.apple.com/quicktime).

Audiovisual formats

Unlike many items of computer software and hardware, there is no standard file format for either sound or video files (the file format is the suffix at the end of the file name, such as .doc for a Word document). Different media players can play different formats, although thankfully there is quite a bit of overlap. Both Media Player and WinAmp play the popular MP3 format, for example. Some of the most common formats are: **.mp3** (audio),

.**mpeg** (video), .**wav** (audio), .**midi** (audio), .**mov** (video), .**avi** (audio video) plus .**rm** and .**ra** (RealPlayer's own video and audio formats respectively). But like the rest of the computer world, technology moves fast, and new file formats are appearing all the time. So don't be too frustrated if you come across the odd one that you can't play or don't recognize.

MP3 files

The best-known audio file format is MP3, which is now becoming the industry standard. MP3s have almost single-handedly revolutionized the music industry, because of the ease with which they can be distributed and stored. It is a sign of just how much PCs and the Web have become integrated into our domestic lives when having to use a computer to obtain your music, rather than buying CDs in a shop, is no longer seen as an obstacle.

What are MP3s?

MP3s (short for Moving Pictures Expert Group Layer 3 – now you know why they're just called MP3s!) are a compressed digital audio file format that allows you to store far more music on your PC than you could, say, by transferring it from a conventional CD. For example, the average pop song would use up around 30MB of space on your PC as a normal CD file, and take about two hours to download from the Web with a standard 56K modem. As an MP3 file, the same song takes up a mere 3MB of space and – the Internet permitting – about twelve minutes to download. In other words, it's ten times smaller.

How do they work?

MP3s achieve their small size by stripping away all the inaudible parts of a digital sound file, leaving a much smaller file. Music purists argue that they are inferior in sound quality to CDs because of this, but judging by their huge popularity, not many people seem to notice.

Why are they so controversial?

Record companies almost had a collective heart attack when they encountered MP3s for the first time. Rather than purchasing their CDs in a shop, computer users could now download the same album free of charge very easily from the Web. The record companies adopted an 'if you can't beat them, join them' approach and agreed legislation that would prohibit the free distribution of the most popular music, without banning MP3s outright. In 2000, the most famous MP3 distribution site, Napster, lost a court case when Sony sued them for millions of dollars in compensation. Napster soldiered on bravely for a while, agreeing to charge users for downloading the music; its file-sharing facility is currently inactive, though the service is still in partial operation. However, record companies have begun to embrace the technology, with artists such as David Bowie releasing albums on the Web, which the buyer has to pay for before downloading. The fear of MP3s now seems to have subsided somewhat, and CD burners and recordable CD players probably pose more of a threat to record company revenue.

What's available on MP3 and where can I get it?

Although the biggest artists are fiercely protected by the record companies, there's a huge catalogue of freely available music (and audio books for that matter) from Mozart to Madonna. Unsigned bands often use it as a way of getting themselves known, releasing a few tracks on MP3 that you can download and listen to free of charge. Even mainstream artists now throw in the odd soundclip from their new album, to give their fans a taste of their latest offering. Here are some of the best MP3 sites around:

MP3 (www.mp3.com)
2000MP3 (www.2000mp3.com)
Audiofind (www.audiofind.com)
Free-MP3s (www.free-mp3s.net)
HitSquad (www.hitsquad.com)
Liquid Audio (www.liquidaudio.com)

MP3 isn't just for music – if you like listening to audio books and newspapers, you can find a selection of MP3 versions at Audible.com (www.audible.com).

Organizing your MP3 collection

If you get the MP3 bug, you'll find your collection builds up very quickly. Why not organize it in a virtual jukebox on your desktop? With an MP3 jukebox, you can organize your collection into themes, create playlists and look up track listings. Two popular jukeboxes are RealJukebox (from www.real.com) and WinAmp Jukebox (www.winamp.com). And you're not just restricted to playing your MP3s on your PC – reasonably priced portable MP3 players are available in the shops (some are even incorporated into mobile phones!), or you can copy them on to a CD-R (recordable CD) with a CD burner.

Image file formats

Many websites offer files of images that you can download. As with audiovisual files, there are a wide range of formats for image (picture) files. Some of the most common are: .bmp (pronounced bitmap), .jpg (jay-peg), .gif (g as in gorilla) and .tif (tiff). Gifs usually have the smallest file sizes but lose image quality because they are more compressed than the others. Tiffs offer the best quality out of the above formats, as they compress files without losing quality, but have much larger file sizes, taking longer to download. A JPEG is often a good compromise as it's somewhere between the two in both size and quality. You may not be given a choice as to which format you want to download the image in, but if you are you need to weigh up file size against picture quality – as with most things in life, it's a trade-off.

Two great sites for downloading free graphics are Free Graphics (www.free-graphics.com) and Free Images (www.freeimages.co.uk). You can also try the amazing The FreeSite (www.freesite.com) – this is actually a directory, listing just about everything that's free on the Web, and one of its sections contains a list of sites with free graphics.

Clipart Graphics is just one site that offers free images

Alternatively, if you just want to download an image that is part of a web page, simply right-click on the image and select 'Save Picture As' from the pop-up menu. Choose a location to save it to (for example, My Documents) and click OK. You can also choose to save an image as wallpaper (the background image on your screen) in this way, by choosing 'Set as Wallpaper' from the same menu.

Animated graphics

Website creators are always looking for ways to make the multimedia experience more entertaining, and animated graphics are a very popular method of achieving this end. If you've ever surfed the Web, you've probably come across moving images – perhaps a plane flying across the sky or a dancing cartoon figure. You're bound to have seen them in various banner ads around the Web too. While such animation is very entertaining, it often requires plug-ins or other software to view it. The site will detect whether you have these already in your browser, and if not, usually offers to download them. Here are three of the most common:

ActiveX

ActiveX is not a plug-in – it's just a set of controls that enables certain types of web animation to be viewed. Because it's written by Microsoft, the company also has helpfully enabled it to link your Microsoft Office programs to the Web. If you have Internet Explorer, this allows you to view Word or Excel documents on a web page through your browser, for example. However, note that ActiveX doesn't work on other browsers.

Shockwave

One of the most popular plug-ins around, Macromedia's Shockwave allows you to access all sorts of multimedia content created with one of its own web-design programs, such as Flash. So much multimedia content on the Web is created in Flash – it's almost an industry standard – that Shockwave has become a vital accessory for surfers. If you haven't got it, you won't be able to view many websites properly. Again, though, most sites will detect whether you already have Shockwave, and will enable you to download it if necessary.

Applets

Applets are mini programs, usually written in the Java programming language, which allow you to view various types of multimedia content. Unlike Shockwave, applets are not permanent – they simply download themselves automatically when they're needed, to view certain Web content, then disappear from your PC when you go offline. The advantage of this is that you don't have to spend time downloading special plug-ins.

The streaming media revolution

Streaming media has revolutionized multimedia content on the Web, because it has enhanced the quality of moving pictures and sound beyond all recognition. 'Streaming' refers to the downloading of data that makes up the audio or video clip, in a steady, continuous stream. This allows your browser to begin playing the clip before it has fully downloaded. It does this in a simple but ingenious way: a go-between, called a streaming client, receives data from the website and passes it on to the media player in your browser (such as RealPlayer). If the client receives data faster than the player can convert it into sound and pictures, it holds the excess data in a temporary storage area called a buffer, until the player has caught up. It then releases more data, so it is always sent in a steady stream. However, the quality of such video clips can be very poor.

Copy it right

Finally, a word of warning about using multimedia images, especially graphics. Make sure you are permitted to use the image before you download it. Most creators allow personal use (i.e. just on your own PC) but using them for commercial purposes or sharing them among your friends may infringe the copyright. If you're not sure, stick to images that are free, and use them just for your own, non-commercial purposes.

Online radio

While there's little point in listening to a radio station online if you can get it on your radio, the Web allows you to listen to stations from all over the world.

Previously, radio programmes were only transmitted by analogue radio waves, but now many stations also transmit their broadcasts in digital format, or have them converted, meaning they can be sent over the Web. RealPlayer, currently the most popular media player available, has a 'Radio' feature allowing you to access hundreds of stations around the globe. Windows Media Player and Winamp have one too. You can surf the airwaves to see what's out there, search by music format (Rock, Country, Classical and so on) or select a specific radio station. Many radio stations also have their own websites, where you can access a broadcast directly – for example Virgin Radio (www.virginradio.co.uk) and Radio 2 (www.bbc.co.uk/radio2). If you have a pay-as-you-go Internet service, however, don't get carried away – it's amazing how the hours can slip by listening to your favourite radio station, while the phone costs mount up.

Games without frontiers

One of the biggest attractions of the Web is playing online games. The Web allows you to find an almost endless supply of opponents for games you are familiar with, and the chance to discover exciting new games to test your skills. Whether you want a relaxing game of cards with a single opponent, or a multi-player shoot-'em-up to save the universe, you can find it all online.

Prepare your PC

If you have a fairly basic PC, which is normally used for word-processing tasks and the odd bit of Web browsing, asking it to suddenly play the most advanced online games is not the best idea – quite frankly, it won't know what's hit it. Most new PCs can easily handle the more basic games, such as chess or cards, but a multi-user role-playing game could be asking too much. So if you want to play the more advanced games, try and use a fast connection speed – broadband Internet access, using ADSL or a cable modem, is ideal as it's many times faster than a conventional phone line. You should also have a fast processor (the faster the better – processors in excess of 1GHz are now available) and lots of RAM – at least 128MB is advisable. You'll also need a 3D graphics card and a good-quality sound card. Many gamers even buy a second PC dedicated solely to game playing, and leave their other computer for more menial tasks, but there's no need to go this far until you're really hooked!

How do online games work?

There are two types of online game: those held on private networks and those on commercial ones. Private games are often free to play, and are at the more traditional end of the market; if you're not familiar with gaming, they're a

Gamespy.com – a private network game site

good place to start. You can access many private network games at Gamespy (www.gamespy.com). Commercial networks, which often host the more spectacular games, are held on special servers on the Internet (powerful central computers with lots of storage space), which you connect to via the Web. Because they attract a more expert crowd, who want serious opponents, commercial networks are often pay-per-play or require a subscription fee to join. They also host huge role-playing games called MMORPGs (Massively Multiplayer Online Role-Playing

Purplelion.com – just one of the free games websites

Games), allowing literally thousands of gamers all over the world to play at once. Popular commercial networks include Heat (www.heat.net) and the MSN Gaming Zone (www.zone.com).

Some games are played in 'real time' – that is, you all access the gaming board over the Web, and each move you make can be seen by the other players simultaneously. Other games 'pass' the board around by downloading it to each player, who then uploads it again when they've made their move. Obviously, the second type is much slower, but at least it gives you more thinking time for those tricky moves. The most basic of all games are often played purely by e-mail, and are not surprisingly called Play by e-Mail (PbeM) games. As a general rule, if you just want a bit of fun, use the private networks, but if you start to get serious and want professional chess or poker opponents, for example, you're better off with the commercial networks.

Listen to the voices

One amazing innovation in online gaming has been the ability to incorporate speech. Roger Wilco (www.resounding.com) is a chat application allowing you to talk to other players in a MMORPG, with the aid of a microphone connected to your PC. Not only does this add realism to a game, it also speeds things up, as talking is obviously a lot faster than typing.

Play by e-mail (PbeM) Games

The simplest PbeMs exclude a board game altogether and are purely text based. Many people play chess in this way – simply e-mailing their moves to each other and adjusting a real board or moves on a piece of paper to keep track. Other e-mail chess games are more sophisticated, passing a board between opponents as a small e-mail attachment or via a website. Many PbeMs are surprisingly complex, involving detailed 'dungeons and dragons'-style role-playing scenarios with many players. This can get a bit cliquey for some, but others get hooked very quickly.

Lurk before you leap

If you do fancy a go at an online game, many sites allow you to watch a game without taking part – a process known as 'lurking'. You'll come across the same word used about chatrooms (see 'Talk Talk'). You can also check out newsgroups (where players discuss issues about the game in question) to get a feel for your opponents and the games themselves. If you fancy joining a role-playing game, why not check out the Godlike gaming site (www.godlike.com/muds), to discover how you can take part.

Downloading games

Of course, you don't have to play all of your games online – you can also download games to play offline, at your leisure. Some of the best game downloads can be found at:

Free Games Online (www.freegamesonline.com)
Games Archives (www.gamesarchives.com)
Free Gaming (www.free-gaming.com)
Game Pod (www.purplelion.com/games)
Yahoo! (www.yahoo.com/recreation/games)

Downloading: the hidden danger

Finally, before you go crazy downloading everything in sight, bear in mind there is a danger that comes with allowing something unknown from the Web onto your PC – viruses. This is covered in more detail in the later chapter 'Look After Yourself', but as a wise precaution, it's highly advisable to install some anti-virus software before you begin downloading software or opening e-mail attachments. One of the most popular is Norton AntiVirus, available from www.symantec.com, and also in many PC stores. Another reputable package is McAfee Virus Scan (www.nai.com).

SHOPPING

After a sluggish start, shopping has become one of the success stories of the Web, and is now one of the most common online activities – it's estimated the UK spends around £10 billion a year shopping in cyberspace. Today, you can buy anything from aromatherapy to airline tickets, horseshoes to houses, and food to fantasy football teams online. The Web is a shopper's paradise, allowing consumers to benefit from a huge range of goods worldwide, cheaper prices than many high-street stores, and the comfort and convenience of ordering from your armchair. But remember – it's your money, so it pays to know your way around.

Where do you start?

You can think of the Web as a global shopping mall, and as such it's handy to have a store guide to point you in the right direction. As we saw in 'The Wonder of the World Wide Web', there are several search engines and directories to guide you to the right sites, and such search facilities abound for online shoppers. Some of the most useful shopping directories include:

> **The All Internet**
>   **Shopping Directory** (www.all-internet.com)
> **Shopping Search** (www.shoppingsearch.com)
> **Yahoo! Shopping** (www.shopping.yahoo.com)
> **I want to shop** (www.iwanttoshop.com)
> **IMRG Shops Directory** (www.imrg.sotn.com)
> **Internet Shopper** (www.internetshopper.com)

There are hundreds of thousands of shops listed on these sites, so you should be able to find something you're after before too long.

What sort of shops are available online?

Anything and everything. With the Web, you have quite literally got the whole shopping world in your hands. The following is a tiny sample of what's out there, but it will give you an idea of the ways that many surfers choose to spend their hard-earned cash.

Books, music and video

Amazon.com – one of the best-known online media sites

One of the first areas to really take off in the world of online shopping, there are now millions of books, computer games, CDs and videos available from various companies. Two of the best known are Amazon (www.amazon.com) and Books Online (www.bol.com). Both sites sell a mind-boggling range of media products, and have been joined by many high-street book and music stores with their own online shops, such as Waterstone's (www.waterstones.co.uk) for books and HMV (www.hmv.co.uk) for music and video. Such online stores can often offer large discounts on their goods, because of the vast stock they can hold in their warehouses, without the overheads of running a high-street shop. Due to their vast range, they can be invaluable for tracking down that elusive early album by a cult artist, or the latest by your favourite author. However, make sure you know how long it will take to deliver your items, and take into account postage costs when comparing them to high-street stores.

Groceries

One of the areas that's seen a surprise growth in the last couple of years is supermarket shopping. Presumably it demonstrates just how little consumers enjoy trundling their trolley round the local supermarket, and how they would much rather have it delivered to home or office for a small fee. It's a godsend for those without transport who can't get to a supermarket, too. They can now benefit from a range of goods that the corner shop just can't match. Most supermarkets will deliver within twelve hours, to home or office, and charge a delivery fee of around £5.00. The organization behind it has to be seen to be believed, with coolboxes, pizza protectors and even wine coolers all used to ensure your produce reaches you in perfect condition. Supermarkets are in a highly competitive business, and it's the consumer that benefits as each tries to outdo the others in price, range and service. Shop around at these supermarket sites:

Tesco (www. tesco.com)
Sainsburys (www.sainsburystoyou.com)
Waitrose (www.waitrose.co.uk)
Asda (www.asda.com)

A word of advice when using supermarket sites: if they haven't got the goods you want in stock, be wary of allowing them to choose a 'suitable alternative'. Such choices have included replacing orange juice with bathroom cleaner in the past, so watch out! Secondly, as you become more familiar with what your favourite supermarket offers, make a shopping list before you start – it's much easier to select items by name, rather than simply choosing 'frozen food' and having to browse through 100 different foodstuffs to find the one you want.

Auction sites

This is a massive growth area in online shopping, although most of the popular auctions seem to be controlled by just a few major sites. Many visitors say it's highly addictive – it's amazing how you just can't live without that 1970s macramé kit once you've seen it at auction! It's more fun to try out the person-to-person sites first (such as eBay and Auctionweiser) although commercial, company auctions also exist. Familiarize yourself with the way that each site works before you jump in with a bid, and choose sites that alert you of any new bids for the items you're interested in, so you don't have to sit glued to the site for the whole time. Some sites, including eBay, will also put in a last-minute bid for you, to save you having to continually bid for the whole time. And don't worry about a long, drawn-out process – some sites, such as First Auction, hold 'flash' auctions that are fixed at 30 minutes, although a standard auction normally takes three days to a week. As with other online shopping, always check out the retail price of the item you want, or go to auctioneer's sites like Sotheby's (www.sothebys.com) to check out the going rate for more unusual items, to ensure it's a fair price. Never send cash for payment – credit cards are ideal, as they automatically protect you against fraud.

Some of the most popular auction sites include:

eBay (www.ebay.com and www.ebay.co.uk)

Auctionweiser (www.auctionweiser.com)

QXL (www.qxl.com)

First Auction (www.firstauction.com)

Edeal (www.edeal.com)

UBid (www.ubid.com)

Airlines

If you'll excuse the pun, discounted airfares have really taken off on the Web, as office workers in need of a break book flights in minutes online that might have taken them half the afternoon to book over the phone or at the local travel agent. Moreover, many airlines offer additional discounts for booking online, as it cuts down their administration costs. Most major airlines now have an online booking facility, and two airlines –

Go and Easy Jet – have proved particularly popular, offering air fares to some destinations that would be far more expensive if booked through more conventional avenues. All online sites tap into one of the four worldwide airline reservation systems to make bookings, so try and check out at least three sites to ensure you get a range of deals. As with a phone or travel agent booking, take precautions by ensuring the company you book with is ABTA- or ATOL-bonded, and that you know precisely the terms and conditions of your booking. Use a credit card, to protect against fraud. Some airlines, such as Easy Jet, even offer a ticketless booking system, e-mailing you a reference number instead, so make sure you know which you're getting. Head for one of these sites for a place in the sun:

Go (www.go-fly.com)

Easy Jet (www.easyjet.com)

Airline Guide (http://the-travel-guide.com)

Expedia.com (www.expedia.com)

The price is right

Before you buy or sell anything online, it pays to check out what various online and high-street stores are charging – you might save yourself a considerable amount. You can do this store by store if you wish, but, as ever, there are websites that will happily do the job for you. Perhaps the best-known of these is ShopSmart (www.shopsmart.com), which gives you a price check on an item in a range of stores, so that you can pick the best deal. If you need more information about products, you could look out for the on-site reviews by previous customers, or check out consumer sites such as Consumer World (www.consumerworld.com) and CompareNet (www.comparenet.com), which will even suggest a range of products that fit your requirements.

Making a payment online

When making a payment over the Web, always apply the golden rule: never make a payment for goods or services online in a situation that you wouldn't be happy about in a shop or over the phone. In other words, apply the same common sense to an online transaction that you would to any other purchase. Wherever possible, use a credit card to make the payment, as you are automatically protected against fraud by doing so, and never send cash. It's advisable to make a paper record of any transactions, too, in case of query – a good practice is to print out any invoices or pages of order details.

How does a credit card payment work?

One of the reasons online shopping got off to such an uncertain start was the understandable reluctance of consumers to give out their credit card details over the Web. But now, with secure payment systems in place on most sites, paying online is actually far safer than paying by phone or in a shop. You'll notice when you make a payment that you're often informed that you're in the secure area of the site, indicated by a padlock icon at the bottom of the screen. When you enter and send your credit card details as instructed, your web browser scrambles the details while they're sent over the Internet, and then the website unscrambles them at the other end – a process known as encryption. The details are encoded to make them almost impossible to read by anyone else – the modern equivalent of coding wartime messages, in a way. One of the most popular (and currently the most secure) programs for doing this is SSL (Secure Sockets Layer).

The website should say somewhere which encryption system it uses. If in any doubt, look for the padlock symbol (as used by Internet Explorer) or occasionally a key (as used by Netscape), which indicates a secure site. While these systems are not foolproof – even Microsoft owner Bill Gates has reputedly had his credit card details exposed by hackers – it's certainly a lot safer than many other methods of payment that you never think twice about.

The small print

Being aware of the terms and conditions of your online purchases should make you more confident about conducting transactions over the Web. Here are some useful points to bear in mind:

1. **Check additional costs** – some companies charge postage and packing, some don't.
2. **Check delivery times** – even if goods are cheaper at one site than another, you may have to wait longer for delivery. Some sites charge extra for next-day delivery. Don't forget you need to be around to receive the goods too – if you can't be at home, plan ahead and arrange for them to be delivered to your work address.
3. **Always read the terms and conditions of the sale**, which should be clearly shown on the site.
4. **If you suffer from 'buyer's remorse'** after making a purchase, you are perfectly entitled to return the goods in their original state, for a refund, usually within a 14- or 28-day period. However, if you buy something from abroad, returning it could be prohibitively expensive, so think carefully before you buy.
5. **Check your warranty.** If you're buying items of hardware, such as a computer, check the terms of the warranty before you buy. You should have at least a

one-year guarantee against faulty manufacture and equipment failure, and if possible go for an on-site warranty, whereby the engineer will come to you, rather than having the hassle of returning your goods for repair. In addition, some online retailers offer their own guarantee against faulty goods, which then passes to the manufacturer after a certain length of time.

6. **Credit card payments protect you against fraud. Debit cards don't.** If you use a credit card to pay for goods that the company subsequently fails to deliver, your credit card company is legally obliged to reimburse you. If you pay by Switch, however, you won't receive the same protection.

UNDERSTANDING
E-MAIL

After discovering some of the wonders of the Web in the previous chapters, it's time to look at one of the Internet's earliest, and most-used features – e-mail. This chapter will show you what it is, how to use it and just why it's become so popular.

What is e-mail?

The term e-mail is short for 'electronic mail', which serves to distinguish it from postal (or what e-mailers occasionally unkindly refer to as 'snail') mail. E-mail takes the form of a typed message, sometimes with a document attached, sent from your PC, across the Internet to the recipient's computer, which can often receive it almost immediately. In a sense, it's halfway between a quick phone call and a letter, although many people prefer to use it instead of either of those (rather old-fashioned!) methods nearly all the time.

How does it work?

Just as websites each have a unique address to ensure your browser finds the right one, so each person's e-mail address is unique too, and the transfer system is similar as well. Whenever you send an e-mail, it is transferred over the Internet to your ISP's outgoing mail server, where it's held until it's ready to be sent to the next link in the chain. Similarly, your ISP's incoming mail server holds all your new mail for you, until you log on to the Internet and retrieve it, via an e-mail program such as Outlook Express. You can then read it at your leisure. Just like a website address, each e-mail address is unique, so that your incoming and outgoing mails are able to find their destination. Let's look at a fictional e-mail address – joebloggs@isp.com – to see how it's constructed.

joebloggs

The username. This is the name that the owner of the address chose for themselves when they signed up with an ISP. In other words, it identifies the person to whom the address belongs, just as you would start off with the person's name on an envelope when sending a conventional letter.

@ISP

ISP is the 'domain' name (sometimes called the 'host' name). This is the name of the company who own or use the mail server on the Internet that sends your mail back and forth. Very often it's the name of the ISP (AOL, Freeserve, Virgin or whatever) that you signed up with to get access to the Net. The @ sign is common to all e-mail addresses, and separates the username from the domain name. It's also an easy way to distinguish an e-mail address from a website address, a distinction that often confuses newcomers.

.com

The domain suffix. This works in the same way as the suffix on a website address. So here, .com suggests the host is a commercial company.

Why is it so popular?

E-mail is probably the most popular form of long-distance communication on the planet. The reason for this is threefold: it's easy to use, it's fast and it's cheap – ideal characteristics for any means of communication. With e-mail you can send a simple typed message or a family photo to Aunt Maud in Australia in a matter of minutes, for a fraction of the cost of normal mail or an expensive long-distance phone call. It costs you no more to send an e-mail than it does to use the Web, as you are using exactly the same technology – a phone line and the Internet – to access both.

In addition, many people find e-mail the ideal compromise between a phone call and a letter. Unlike a phone call, you can write down exactly what you want to say, giving you time to phrase it and so avoid any verbal misunderstandings. Yet it has the permanency of a written letter – it can be stored on a computer or printed out, and both sender and receiver get a copy of it, which avoids any dispute over what was said. What's more, unlike a letter, it can often reach the recipient in a matter of minutes, saving valuable time. E-mail has become so popular that many office workers find it is their favoured form of communication – even if the other person is in the same office!

How do I use e-mail?

If you've already set up your Internet access, through your ISP, you're halfway there. Many ISPs configure your e-mail automatically, so you may find it's running already. Now all you need is an e-mail reader program, such as Outlook Express, and an e-mail address through your ISP. Most ISPs offer at least one free address, and many offer several, so each member of your family can have their own. There are also Web-based e-mail accounts available, but we'll look at those later.

Setting up your e-mail account

If you've bought a PC in the last few years, and are using Windows 98 or Me, you'll have Outlook Express (or Outlook) pre-installed. It's by far the most popular e-mail reader around, although other popular programs include Messenger (part of Netscape Communicator) and the early e-mail program Eudora. Windows makes setting up an e-mail account easy, so here's how to do it with Outlook Express:

1. Double-click on the Internet Connection Wizard icon on your desktop. In the box that appears, type in your name as you would like it to appear in the 'From' box when you send an e-mail (this does not have to be the same as your username – you can choose a nickname if you prefer). Click Next.

2. Now enter your e-mail address. This will be assigned by your ISP, so contact them if you're unsure. You can usually choose your own username (providing that someone else hasn't got it already). The ISP's name will usually follow after the @ symbol. Then click Next.

3. Enter the names of your ISP's e-mail servers. These are the powerful computers that handle your incoming and outgoing mail – a bit like a huge postal depot. Again, contact your ISP for these details if you don't know them. Incoming mail is handled by a POP3 (Post Office Protocol 3) or the newer IMAP (Internet Message Access Protocol) server. Outgoing mail is handled by an SMTP (Simple Mail Transport Protocol). Click Next.

4. Finally, enter the username and password that you

use to access the Internet. If you click 'Remember password', from now on Outlook Express will retrieve your e-mails without asking you to enter your password each time. Now simply click Finish and the connection wizard tells you that your e-mail account has been set up successfully. Congratulations! Now you're ready to send and receive e-mails.

Using Outlook Express – the basics

Here are the main tools on your toolbar for handling your e-mail:

New Mail

Click this button when you want to open a new mail. Then type your message, giving it a heading if you wish, and carefully type in the e-mail address of the recipient. Finally, click the Send button.

Send/Recv

This tells Outlook Express to connect to your ISP's incoming/outgoing mail servers on the Net, then download any incoming messages and send any outgoing mail.

Reply

Opens a new window to allow you to type a reply to the sender of the selected e-mail. Once you have done so, click Send.

Reply All

Be extremely careful with this one! Reply All sends your reply to all the people to whom the selected mail was originally sent, and not just to the sender of the e-mail that you received yourself. Many's the time that an intimate or confidential reply has been mailed to the whole office in error, because Reply All was clicked instead of Reply!

Forward

Lets you send a received message to someone else, including any attachments that came with the e-mail.

Address

Opens the Address Book, where you can add and retrieve the e-mail addresses and details of all your contacts. If you want to add someone's e-mail address to your book quickly, without having to type it, simply select an incoming message from that person, go to the Tools menu and click on 'Add to Address Book'. Their e-mail address is now in your Address Book.

Find

Allows you to search for a particular e-mail by sender, subject header or message contents. Very handy

 when you're trying to track down an elusive e-mail in an overflowing inbox.

Print

As it suggests, simply click this button to print out your selected e-mail.

Web-based e-mail

An even simpler way to get hooked up to e-mail is to use an account based on a website rather than a POP3 server. Web-based e-mail accounts have the advantage that you can pick up your mail from anywhere with Web access, rather than having to be stationed at your own PC. However, they can be less user-friendly, and if the website is down for any reason, you won't be able to get your mail. They often restrict the size of any attachments you can include too (usually to 1MB), and simply won't deliver it if it's any larger. But they are undoubtedly useful if you're always on the move. Many

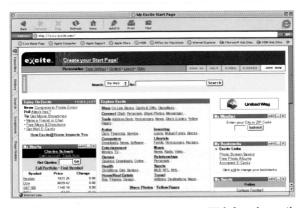

At Excite.com, you can set up your own Web-based e-mail

people get the best of both worlds, by having a POP3 account and a Web-based account for when they're away from their desk. If you're going to do this, just remember to tell people which e-mail address to use when. Some Web-based e-mail now provides a POP3 service too. Here are some of the most popular Web-based e-mail sites – simply follow the instructions on the website to set up an account:

Hotmail (www.hotmail.com)
Yahoo! (www.yahoo.co.uk)
Excite (www.excite.com)
Name Planet (www.nameplanet.com)
iName (www.iname.com)
Ecosse (www.ecosse.net)

Talking E-mail

If you'd prefer to take a break from your screen, or are
visually impaired, you can also have your incoming mail
read out to you. Talking E-mail is an e-mail reader that
links up with your normal e-mail program, and uses the
Office assistant characters familiar to Word and Excel
to read out your messages in a friendly fashion.
Obviously, you'll need speakers on your PC to hear
them, but it can be a very handy (and unusual!) way of
receiving your mail. The program also uses the Office
assistants to read out a time check if you wish, and
they'll read out any text pasted onto your Windows
clipboard from a standard document, too, so you can

listen for errors. A free trial version of Talking E-mail is available at www.4dev.com/talkmail.

Attachments

An attachment is simply a document sent in an e-mail that is not part of the message itself. You can think of it as the e-mail equivalent of enclosing a photo with a letter sent by normal mail. Attachments make e-mail even more handy by allowing documents to be sent quickly over long distances via the Net. They are perfect for enhancing the content of your message, or for illustrating your point. Most e-mail programs make sending or receiving attachments very easy indeed.

Sending an attachment

To include a file such as a Word document, a photo or a soundclip with an e-mail in Outlook Express, simply click on the paperclip in the New Message window. From the list of documents that appears, click the one you wish to include, then click Attach. Now simply click Send to mail it. Most POP3 accounts will tolerate

A standard e-mail layout, showing space for attachments

file sizes up to about 3.5MB, but these can be very slow to send. If you have files over about 1MB, it's a good idea to compress them first, using a compression program like WinZip (www.winzip.com). This can reduce their file size by up to 60 per cent in some cases. If you wish to send pictures, which are far larger than the average text document, open them in Paint Shop Pro (or a similar graphics program) and re-save them in a compressed file format such as a JPEG (see 'Multimedia: Software, Sound and Vision'). The picture quality will be slightly worse, but at least it won't take forever to send.

Receiving an attachment

In Outlook Express, you can tell if the e-mail you've received has an attachment, by whether or not it has a paperclip next to it in your inbox. To access the attachment, open the e-mail, see what the attachment is about, then click the paperclip once you're sure it's safe to open. The attachment will now open automatically, or a pop-up menu will appear asking you to choose which program you'd like to use to open the attachment (such as Word). Never open an attachment that you're not sure about – it could contain a virus. Program files (such as those ending with .exe) are more likely to contain viruses than text or image files, but it's better to be safe then sorry. Even many experienced e-mail users forgot this golden rule when they received the famous 'I Love You' attachment. Unable to resist such a tempting titbit, they opened the attachment – and proceeded to find out just how much it loved them as it destroyed much of their hard disk and spread to other computers. Because of such dangers, several e-mail programs, including Outlook Express, ask you if you want to open the file in your browser or save it first to your hard disk. If you're in any doubt, always save it, as this will help protect you from any virus. See 'Look After Yourself' for more on virus protection.

Why can't I open an attachment?

Most text files, such as Word and Excel documents, should be straightforward to open because your PC already has these programs installed on it. Most e-mail can be converted to the MIME (Multipurpose Internet Mail Extensions) format for sending, including the attachment itself. MIME can be read by most e-mail programs. However, if an attachment won't open it's probably either because your PC hasn't got a suitable program to open it, or because the attachment itself has become corrupted (damaged) en route. Graphics (picture) and multimedia files can be a bit trickier as there are a wide variety of file formats (see 'Multimedia:

Software, Sound and Vision') and your PC may not have a program – or programs – that can open them all. Windows 98 and Me come with a basic graphics program called Paint, but this is only able to handle a limited number of file formats. You may want to invest in a program like the versatile Paint Shop Pro (available from many computer stores and www.jasc.com), which can open over 30 different graphics file formats. As a last resort, you can try opening a picture file as part of a Word document. Right-click on the file, choose Save as and click OK. Now open Word, click the Insert menu and choose Picture, then From File. Locate the picture you just saved from the list that appears and double-click it, to see if it will open. However, if your PC doesn't even attempt to open a file, the attachment could be corrupt, so ask the sender to e-mail it to you again.

TALK TALK

There is nowhere quite like the Internet for freedom of expression. The Web itself is a vast, unstructured network of sites, many created by individuals with something to say, or an interest to pursue. E-mail allows you to reach people directly, even on the other side of the world, to voice your opinion. The third area of the Internet that encourages this is somewhere between the two – group discussion. There is a huge array of newsgroups, chatrooms and message boards on the Net, allowing people to share their thoughts with groups of others, exchange ideas and find like-minded people for even the most obscure interests. Whatever you're into, you can share your passion in all sorts of ways, with group discussion over the Net.

How does group discussion work?

Although you can access many group discussion facilities via websites and plain old e-mail, the facilities themselves are held on special servers on the Internet. So when you access a group discussion facility, you are accessing one of these servers, not the Web. The principle behind group discussion is that you can contact a group of people simultaneously, and you in turn will be contacted simultaneously by the rest of the group, with any replies. Some facilities, such as chatrooms, operate in 'real time' – you can view a message in the chatroom as soon as it's sent, and your reply will appear instantly too. Others, like message boards, operate more like e-mail, with a slight delay time – it may take a while for your message to appear on the board and for any replies to appear too.

Message boards

Message or 'bulletin' boards are one of the most simple but effective forms of online discussion. Unlike newsgroups, you don't need additional software to use them – just a simple registration process, which often allows you access to several boards on the same server. Although they don't operate in real time, the messages generally appear very quickly, and the debates can become very intense at times. One popular use of message boards is through sports club websites, to give fans a voice.

Check out the Rivals website (www.rivals.net) for a host of different sporting sites with message boards.

Newsgroups

A newsgroup is simply a discussion area on the Net, and so the word 'news' is a bit misleading – although people may be discussing the latest events surrounding a topic, they could be discussing anything else to do with the subject as well. Users 'post' (send electronically) their messages to the newsgroup server for everyone to read, and a discussion can then begin, when other users post their comments/replies to the original message. At its best, it's a wonderful source of information on just about any topic you wish – there may be thousands of other users with a similar interest to you, all keen to give you free opinions and advice (perhaps a bit too keen sometimes!) whenever you need them. And you can feel virtuous, or at least sociable, by helping others out in return.

Usenet is a system of dedicated servers devoted to newsgroups. It started life in 1979 as a way of aiding discussion between two Californian universities; now it enables millions of people to chat right round the world.

Accessing a newsgroup

To access a newsgroup on the Net, you'll need some software called a newsreader. The reader acts as a go-between for your PC and the news server. Fortunately, Microsoft has anticipated the need for such newsreaders, and includes one as part of Outlook Express. If you haven't got one, however, you can download one such as Agent (available from www.forteinc.com). Your ISP will usually have its own news server, which your reader can access to see a list of all the different newsgroups it carries. To do this, you need to tell your newsreader the address of your ISP's news server – a very similar process to setting up your e-mail (see 'Understanding E-mail'). If it's not already entered in your newsreader, ask your ISP for its news server address – it will usually be something like 'news.nameofisp.net'.

Once you've set up your newsreader in this way, you can download the list of newsgroups from the news server and choose which ones you want to subscribe to. Subscription is free in most cases – it's just a way of telling your reader which groups you want to read – and you can protect your anonymity with an alias if you wish (many

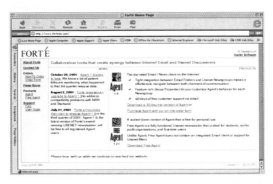

Newsreaders, such as Forteinc's Agent, are easy to download

people do). A list of newsgroups you've subscribed to now appears in your reader – simply click the desired name in the list and you're on your way.

Newsgroup categories

Newsgroups are organized into the following broad subject areas, to help you find what you're looking for. You can click on one of the categories to find a sub-category that interests you:

Comp. Computers and technology

Humanities. The arts, such as music, literature, and philosophy

News. The news service of Usenet

Rec. Pastimes, hobbies, leisure pursuits

Sci. Scientific research and computer science

Soc. Social issues involving culture, religion and lifestyle

Alt. Alternative, or slightly more wacky interests

Misc. Any topics that don't fit into the other categories

Note that an ISP doesn't carry every newsgroup on its server, just a selection, so you may need to search other news servers if you can't find something of interest. You can also access newsgroups through websites, such as Deja (www.deja.com) or HotBot (www.hotbot.com).

Chatrooms

The term chatroom describes its function very well. It refers to a 'room' (albeit in cyberspace) set up for people to visit and have a chat about a particular subject with other like-minded visitors. You can imagine each room with a sign above the door, informing the visitor of the subject being discussed inside. The visitor can stroll round the corridors until they find one to their liking, then enter the room, start a conversation or join an existing one. When they've had enough, they can leave the room, and either 'go home' or visit another chatroom. The great thing about chatrooms is that you can talk in real time – your messages and any replies are displayed in the chatroom instantly, and everyone can view them simultaneously.

How to use a chatroom

To enter a chatroom, you first need to obtain some special software, called a client, to allow you to send and receive messages. It usually consists of three windows – one for typing your messages, one showing the messages of all the other participants, and a third showing a list of current participants. The most common software is called IRC (Internet Relay Chat), a program that's been around since the 1980s. You can download a user-friendly Windows version of IRC from mIRC (www.mirc.com) – simply click the 'Download mIRC' link on the website. As with newsreaders, you need to set up your IRC client to recognize the chatroom server, and again you can choose an 'online identity' to maintain your anonymity. Now you're ready to locate some chatrooms. If you're using mIRC, click the lightning bolt or choose Connect from the File menu. A list of chatrooms (called IRC channels) appears – simply click on one that interests you, and finally click Join. The others in the chatroom will see that you have 'entered' the room. Somebody may welcome you soon afterwards, but if not you can just watch for a while,

Fancy a bit of garden talk? Try Yahoo! 's chatroom page . . .

to get a 'feel' for the room, then introduce yourself with a polite message. Join in the chat as much as you wish, but be polite and don't forget to say goodbye when you leave – the chatroom informs participants automatically when someone has entered or left the room but if a participant misses your exit, they may think you're just ignoring them, so a farewell message is best.

Trying different chatrooms

You can access different chatrooms, on different servers, by going to the File menu and clicking on Setup. A list of chatroom servers will appear, so simply click one to see what it offers. You can also find new chatrooms on websites. The IRC Chat Directory (www.liszt.com/chat) lets you search for new chatrooms, and view a list of the Top 100 in case you're stuck for inspiration.

Web-based chatrooms

If you don't want to go to the bother of downloading IRC software to chat, you can use one of the Web-based chatrooms instead. Some of these require a small applet program to be downloaded first (see 'Multimedia: Software, Sound and Vision'), but this is done automatically so it's very straightforward. Then just follow the website's instructions on how to take part in a chat. A good place to look for Web-based chatrooms is the Yahoo! chatroom directory (http://dir.yahoo.com/ Computers_and_Internet/Internet/World_Wide_Web /Chat/). Many websites also house groups of chatrooms – try Excite (www.excite.com) for starters. Channel 4's chatroom (www.channel4.com/talk) often has celebrity guests from its own shows.

Advanced chatting

If all that typing into a plain old box isn't really your idea of an exciting chat, why not try one of the alternatives?

1. Graphical chat

Some chatroom software allows avatars (fun cartoons that represent your persona online) to be used for chatting. You can even move your avatar around the screen to signify chatting to different people. Your message appears in a speech bubble from your avatar, and bubbles appear from other avatars as they reply. It certainly adds a hint of realism, and a lot more fun, to the proceedings. Try Excite Chat (www.excite.com/communities/chat), which has access to lots of chatrooms and a user-friendly graphical chat program.

2. Video chat

Some advanced software allows you to have a video chat through a webcam or just talk through a microphone attached to your PC, and is becoming increasingly popular. One of the simplest to use is Eyeball (www.eyeball.com). You'll need a webcam and a microphone attached to your PC, but the extra effort can be really worthwhile. The only drawback is that current technology limits you to one-to-one chatting, although group video chats can only be a matter of time. Windows 98 and Me come with video software called NetMeeting, and although it's intended for business use, there's nothing to stop you using it for a friendly chat instead.

Instant messaging

If you prefer talking one-to-one, perhaps just to people you know, you can use another form of chat called instant messaging. Special messaging software detects when any of your friends/family have logged on to the Internet (as long as they're using the same messaging software) and allows you to chat with them in a private chatroom. The most popular instant messaging program is called ICQ (I Seek You), which is available from www.icq.com. Other popular messaging software includes AOL Instant Messenger (www.aol.com/aim), which comes with Netscape Communicator, and Microsoft's MSN Messenger (messenger.yahoo.com).

Netiquette

One of the most important things to remember when communicating with others over the Internet is your manners. It's all too easy to hide behind your computer and deliberately insult someone because you don't have to speak to them in person. But it's just as easy to annoy

Yahoo!'s Messenger – for chatroom privacy

someone unintentionally, because you're unaware of the code of conduct that is used among the group. For this reason, a set of unofficial rules has been drawn up called Netiquette (short for Internet etiquette), to help people get along. As well as these general guidelines, each newsgroup or chatroom may have its own code of conduct, so it's worth checking this out when you visit one for the first time.

It pays to be polite! Here are the basic dos and don'ts of online communication:

1. **Lurk before you leap.** Before diving in with an opinion in an unfamiliar chatroom or newsgroup, simply read what's going on for a while first – a technique known as 'lurking'. This will give you a feel for the tone of the group and enable you to fit in better when you do join in. Use an alias when you join in (it's quite normal to do this) to protect your anonymity, and make you feel more relaxed.

2. **Read the FAQs.** Before asking a question, check the list of FAQs (Frequently Asked Questions) that accompany the chatroom or newsgroup. This will prevent you asking 'old chestnuts' and annoying experienced users with questions they've seen a hundred times before. It's just courteous to find out a bit about the group before you join it.

3. **Avoid a war of words.** Using abusive or insulting language towards another participant is known as 'flaming' (because it's inflammatory) and is considered very bad manners. There is usually one participant who enjoys winding up the rest, who will often make a provocative comment just to ignite the spark. If you find yourself getting caught in such a row, just back out

for a while, and let things calm down. The flamer will often get their comeuppance from another participant.

4. **Don't shout!** WRITING MESSAGES IN CAPITALS is known as shouting and overdoing it will quickly annoy people. Only use capitals when they are necessary, and are not likely to cause offence.

5. **Don't flood the room.** 'Flooding' means repeating the same question over and over or just writing reams of waffle. Try to be as concise as you can, and keep to the subject in hand.

6. **Don't send spam.** Spam is the e-mail equivalent of junk mail. So don't forward any adverts promising instant lottery wins and unmissable offers – they won't be appreciated.

7. **Be nice to newbies.** After you've become a little more experienced, don't forget that newcomers (newbies) still need help. Everyone's a newbie when they start, so show some patience and help them get the hang of things. If you can answer their question, do so – it'll make them feel included in the group, and they may be able to answer one of yours.

8. **Say hello, wave goodbye.** Don't forget the

customary greetings and farewells when you enter and leave a chatroom. Act as if you've met these people in the street, and don't forget to say goodbye when you leave – otherwise they might not realize you've left the room and think you're just rudely ignoring them.

Emoticons

Despite your best efforts, you can still cause offence with various forms of online communication through simple misunderstanding. The written message is a useful tool, but it lacks the facial expression or tone of voice that goes with talking in person, and it's easy for messages to be misconstrued. To help solve this problem, Internet users sometimes accompany their messages with other symbols, called emoticons, to convey the emotion or tone of voice intended. The most widely used emoticons are:

:-) A smile – I'm happy or I'm joking
:-(A frown – I'm sad or cross
;-) A wink – I'm being cheeky or suggestive
❴❵ A hug – I need reassuring, or I'm reassuring you

Although such symbols may seem just a bit of fun, they can be very handy for getting your comment across without causing offence, in any sort of informal communication on the Net. Alternatively, some participants write their reactions/emotions out in full – for example, 'I'm laughing' or 'I'm smiling' – to give an accurate impression.

LOOK

AFTER

YOURSELF

One of the main reasons newcomers to the Net are reluctant to use it is a fear of Big Brother. Confidentiality and security is important to most of us in our daily lives, and that extends to using the Internet. With a bit of insider knowledge, and a bit of forward planning, you can keep your personal life personal, and surf the Net in safety.

What are the security risks of using the Internet?

When you connect to the Net, you are using a gateway between your PC and the servers on the Internet. You can think of it as opening a door on your PC through which all manner of information and visitors can pass. It's up to you when you open that door, and who or what you let through it. It's not just about you visiting the Internet – it's about others using the Internet to visit your PC. You'll find that the security issues that face you over the Net are much the same as those that face you in your everyday life.

The four main security issues are:

1. **Confidentiality** – preventing our e-mails and

information we have given to websites, including
credit card details, being abused by others.

2. **Authenticity** – ensuring that people and companies
   that we contact or that contact us via the Net are
   actually who they say they are.

3. **Protecting children** – preventing access to
   unsuitable material on websites, and via e-mail and
   discussion groups.

4. **Viruses** – malicious programs, transported via e-mail
   or downloads, that are meant to cause damage to
   your PC.

What can you do about it?

A few simple steps, a bit of common sense and regular
vigilance can go a long way to making your experience on
the Net a safe and enjoyable one. Let's take each of the
security issues in turn.

1. Confidentiality

No sooner have you signed up for service or product on
the Web than you receive junk e-mails from a company

you've never heard of, promising you 'the chance of a lifetime'. So how do they get hold of your details?

The way the cookie crumbles

When you give out your details online, the site or service you visited packages the information into a small text file, known as a 'cookie', and asks your PC to store it on your hard drive, which it does by default. When you visit the site again, your PC returns the cookie to the server and personalizes some details on the website for your benefit. It's all very nice to be greeted with 'Hello Mr Smith, welcome to our website again', but the system can be abused. Others can access the information on the cookie, including your e-mail address, and use it for their own ends. Disreputable companies may also pass on your details to other companies without your permission.

You can delete existing cookies in Internet Explorer, by going to Windows Explorer in your Start menu, and selecting the Temporary Internet Files folder. Right-click on the cookie's offending website address in the Name column, and then click on Delete. You can also prevent further cookies being sent to your PC in future. Go to the

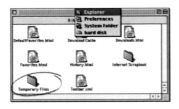

Tools menu in Internet Explorer, and select Internet Options. Click the Security tab, make sure Internet is selected, then go down the list to the Cookies section. Click the button next to Disable (to block all cookies) or Prompt (to give you the option of accepting a cookie each time). Remember – cookies aren't programs so they can't carry viruses – it's the information they carry about you that can be abused. If you'd like to learn more about these intriguing text files, visit Cookie Central at www.cookiecentral.com.

Stop that spam!

One of the negative side-effects of the Internet's ease of communication is that a lot of unwanted mail can reach you. Junk e-mail, or 'spam' as it's known (allegedly because, like the meat product, it's mass-produced, uninteresting and nobody wants it, although its derivation also owes something to a Monty Python sketch in which Spam is an ingredient in every dish on the menu) can appear in your inbox in droves, promising you the world and annoying you intensely. Companies that pass on your details to other companies without your knowledge have a lot to answer for in this process. You may find some spam useful – for example, news of a sale at your favourite online store, or some last-minute flight bargains, but generally it's a nuisance. Here are some ways you can stop that spam:

1. When giving your details to a website, check their privacy policy – make sure they won't pass on your details to a third party, and tick any relevant boxes to request no advertising be sent to you.

2. Block persistent spammers with your e-mail program. In Outlook Express, go to the Inbox, select Organize and click Junk E-mail. Now simply highlight a spam e-mail, go to the Actions menu and select Junk E-mail. Click Add to Junk Senders List. Any further mail from that sender will be blocked. You can also block e-

mails containing certain phrases such as 'Chance of a Lifetime' in the Filter menu of Outlook Express.

3. For more protection, use spam-killing software, such as SpamKiller (www.spamkiller.com) or SpamBuster (www.contactplus.com/spam/spam.htm). These offer a more sophisticated way of dealing with spam than your e-mail program.

4. Get the latest news. JunkBusters (www.junkbusters.com) has the latest information on spam that's doing the rounds. It even provides text that you can send back to the spammer, although replying to spammers is not to be recommended . . .

5. Don't encourage spammers by replying to them – some spam is aimed purely at winding you up. Similarly, don't ask to be removed from their list – you're actually just letting them know you're there and they'll probably start spamming even more.

Shopping with confidence

Online shopping got off to a slow start (several slow starts, actually) as people were very reluctant to give out their credit card details in such a public domain. Their caution may have been well founded at the start, but online security systems are now so advanced that using your credit card on the Net is far safer than using it over the phone or through the post. This is because your details are scrambled as they pass through cyberspace – a process known as encryption – and unscrambled only when they reach their destination. The most common encryption software is called SSL (Secure Sockets Layer) and the most powerful version uses 128-bit encryption, encoding your details using a combination of 128 bits of data.

We've already covered the main precautions you should take when purchasing anything online in 'Shopping Online'. Here are a couple of additional pieces of advice that it's worth bearing in mind.

1. Check the authenticity of the site (see Authenticity below).

2. Check the web page on which you are entering your details is secure – a secure page displays a locked padlock icon (or sometimes a key), and will usually inform you that you are entering a secure part of the site. If you make yourself aware of which parts of a site

are secure and which are not, you'll feel a lot more confident about using it. You can set your browser to warn you when you switch between secure /insecure mode. In Internet Explorer, go to the Tools menu, and select Internet Options, then click the Advanced tab. Scroll down to the Security section and tick the box marked 'Warn if changing between secure and not secure mode'.

Remaining incognito

An easy way of preventing unwanted snoopers is to remain under cover. You can use an anonymous proxy server (so that prying eyes can't tell where the original website request or e-mail came from). A well-known proxy service is Anonymizer (www.anonymizer.com), which keeps your e-mail address and your surfing habits a secret. Such services are also useful when using chatrooms and sending e-mails: they can strip away the header (the blurb showing your username, e-mail address and so on) from any messages that you send, making you anonymous. If you have sensitive information to e-mail around, think about using free encryption software such as PGP (Pretty Good Privacy), available from the PGP site at www.pgpi.org. This will encrypt your e-mails and only allow them to be opened by a person with the correct decryption key at the other end.

2. Authenticity

The Internet can bring people together from all over the world – very often without them having a clue who the people they are communicating with online are. For this reason, it's important to feel that any people you deal with are who they say they are. Here are some things to look out for:

1. **Look for a physical mailing address and a phone number** (not just a PO box number) when you visit a company website for the first time, and check them out.

2. **Check the web address carefully.** Some fraudsters are very adept at creating websites that have similar addresses to well-known ones. So look out for hyphens and dots in the wrong places.

3. **Look for a kitemark certificate**, by a scheme such

as Veri Sign (Microsoft approved) or Web Trader (Consumers' Association approved). The kitemark, also called a digital authentication certificate, means a website has been checked out for authenticity and security. Note that you will have to double-click on the padlock or key symbol to see the certificate.

4. **Do your research.** Before trusting a website, visit some fraud-alert sites such as Internet Scambusters (www.scambusters.org) or Internet Fraud Watch (www.fraud.org) to see if they've uncovered anything of concern about the site. Also check with the governing body of that type of business such as the FSA (Financial Services Authority) for investments (www.thecentralregister.co.uk).

5. **Try and use sites that confirm your order by e-mail.** These usually include a unique order number and a tracking facility, so you can follow the progress of your order. You can visit computer retailer Jungle (www.jungle.com) to see how this works.

6. **Only give out your credit card/personal details in a secure area**. Most websites advertise their security very highly, so if they haven't got any, avoid

them. Never send your bank details/credit card number to the company through the post – several scams have occurred by a company promising to deposit money in the visitor's account in return for sending their bank details. Of course, just the opposite happens – the money is stolen instead.

7. **Ask a friend.** If you want to shop on the Web, get recommendations from friends and family about trusted sites.

8. **Follow the paper trail.** Print out details of your order, the company's guarantee and any other small print, as website content can change very quickly. Much Internet fraud revolves around conditions that never existed, and subscriptions that refuse to cancel. The more physical evidence you can amass, the stronger your position in case of fraud.

3. Protecting children

The Internet provides access to all sorts of material, some of which you certainly don't want your kids to see. As with other media, such as TV or magazines, make sure children are supervised at all times when using the Net.

Content-filtering software

It's reassuring to know the Net can give you a helping hand with child supervision. There are several content-filtering software packages around that allow you to set varying levels of access for different types of content.

Worried about your child and the Net? Try the Net Nanny

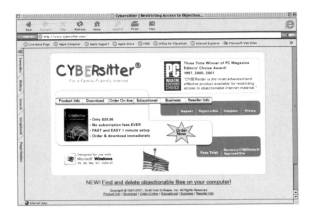

Cybersitter (www.cybersitter.com) is an 'intelligent' filter program that analyzes the context of potentially unsuitable words before blocking them. For example, content featuring 'naked girl' would be blocked but 'the naked eye' would not, allowing child-friendly material to be viewed. Other popular filtering packages include Net Nanny (www.netnanny.co.uk) and Cyber Patrol (www.cyberpatrol.co.uk). The latter also filters e-mail and chatroom content and records any attempts to view unsuitable sites.

Chatroom abuse

It's a sad fact of life, but there are always adults who will misuse the Web, in particular chatrooms, to draw in vulnerable children. Some are highly skilled at gaining the child's confidence first, before moving on to undesirable conversations. Because of this, you should monitor chatroom use by your children extremely carefully. If possible, encourage them to use kids' chatrooms – Freezone (www.freezone.com) offers five monitored, child-friendly chatrooms.

Block it with your browser

A somewhat less sophisticated way of ensuring adult material doesn't reach your child's innocent eyes is through your browser. Internet Explorer allows you to screen content for violence, sex, nudity and explicit language. Go to the Tools menu, select Internet Options, then Content, and click Enable. Now set your ratings as you wish.

Search in safety

There are also child-friendly search engines available, which only allow access to suitable material. Ask Jeeves for Kids (www.ajkids.com) allows children to search the Web in an easy way, and only directs them to child-friendly sites. There are plenty of children's sites around too – one of the best is Yahooligans (www.yahooligans.co.uk), the kids' area of the Yahoo! site.

Software is no substitute

Despite the wide range of filtering software available, it should never be regarded as a substitute for proper supervision. Where possible, use the Net alongside your child, and always be aware of what they are viewing. Adult websites and group discussion areas of the Internet (see 'Talk Talk') pose a particular risk, so never let your child become involved in an interactive activity that you haven't approved. Set your child some rules for Internet use, and make sure they follow them. You can get further advice from the FBI's 'A Parent's Guide to Internet Safety'. Go to www.fbi.gov, then click the

Parents and Teachers link under the FBI for Kids section on the home page.

4. Viruses

The Internet is the largest source of viruses around. Viruses are malicious programs that replicate themselves and cause damage to your computer in some way. Some are relatively harmless while others can destroy your entire hard disk and those of your contacts in your e-mail address book. They can spread easily via e-mail and downloads from the Web.

Is it a bug or a virus?

Before going any further it's worth distinguishing between a bug and a virus. A bug is simply a glitch or unforeseen problem in a program, that the programmer will try and fix. A virus is a malicious program intended to cause damage. For example, the 'Millennium Bug' was a programming problem with the last two digits of the date, but Melissa was a virus that spread rapidly via e-mail, erasing and corrupting computer files.

What are the different types?

There are five main virus types that you may be unfortunate enough to catch. These are:

1. **Parasitic.** Also known as file-infecting viruses, these lurk inside a program then infect other programs and the workings of your PC when you run it.

2. **Worms.** These spread copies of themselves over computer networks, such as the ones used to link up office computers. The first major worm, the 1988 Internet Worm, multiplied to thousands of computers in a few days.

3. **Polymorphic.** Viruses that attempt to evade detection by changing their form as they spread.

4. **Trojan horse.** Any program disguised as (or in) another program to mask its purpose, which is often to spread a virus or install programs that allow the originator to control your PC. Technically not viruses – as they don't replicate – Trojan horses hide inside programs, especially games, and display annoying messages or destroy files.

5. **Script viruses.** These are written in programming languages like VBScript or JavaScript. They can hide

inside an e-mail, and spread when they are unwittingly opened by a visitor. Some older versions of Outlook still allow these.

What can you do to protect yourself?

1. **Install anti-virus software.** Before receiving any e-mail attachments or Internet downloads, you should install a reputable anti-virus program, available from the Web or a high-street retailer. These can be set up to run in the background, continually checking for viruses, destroying present ones and shielding you from new ones. You can also get regular free updates for your program from the manufacturer's website. Some of the most popular versions are:

Norton AntiVirus (www.symantec.com)
McAfee VirusScan (www.mcafee.com)
Command Anti Virus (www.commandcom.com)

2. **Consider 'all-in-one' programs.** Bearing in mind the other risks from the Internet discussed in this chapter, you may want to go for all-in-one virus and security protection. McAfee's Internet Guard Dog Pro (www.mcafee.com) guards against unsuitable web content, security threats, and chatroom abuse, as well as destroying viruses. Another good choice is Norton's Internet Security (the latest version is called 2002) from www.symantec.com.

3. **Check the source.** Never open an e-mail attachment if you don't know who it's from. Viruses are carried in the attachment itself, not the e-mail message, so if you don't open it, you're safe. However, anti-virus software can soon check an e-mail attachment and give you the all-clear.

4. **Open unknown Word documents in another program** like WordPad. The macro viruses (those carried by programming instructions embedded in a document) can only run in Word and so are harmless in WordPad.

5. **Check anti-virus websites for the latest news.** Visit the Symantec AntiVirus Research Centre

(www.symantec.com/avcenter) or check out Wild List (www.wildlist.org), which has a complete list of known viruses, updated monthly.

6. **Heed the warning signs.** If your computer runs slowly or often crashes, you may have a virus. Programs may take longer than normal to load, and devices may stop working properly. You may also get strange messages popping up, such as 'You are surrounded' or 'Your computer is stoned'. If so, run a virus check with some anti-virus software immediately.

What's being done about it?

Viruses have been taken more seriously since 1998, as this was the first time that they started to affect businesses. Previously, they only hit university and college computers. Now, around eighty Computer Emergency Response Teams (CERTs) have been set up by governments and businesses around the globe to tackle the problem worldwide. It's their job to find solutions to viruses when they strike, and try and prevent new ones. Both the FBI and the UK's National Criminal Intelligence Service (NCIS) investigate (and prosecute) several virus and security cases every year. Major viruses are far more likely to affect office networks than home computers, but it's always wise to be cautious by staying vigilant and keeping up to speed with the latest virus developments.

SUPER

SURFING

A modern marvel though it is, the Web can sometimes be a frustrating place to visit – it's often affectionately known as 'the World Wide Wait'. All sorts of factors can affect your surfing experience, and understanding what you can do about them will help to reduce your frustration. This final chapter shows you some of the new technology available and ways to fine-tune your PC to speed up your surf through cyberspace.

The broadband revolution

The most important factor in surfing the Web is how fast that PC of yours can receive and send data down your phone line. A 56Kbps modem sounds fast, but in practice they never work at full speed, and can rarely transfer faster than 49K. But broadband is changing all that.

What is broadband?

Broadband is a term for various types of telecommunications technology. It's so called because it has a broad bandwidth – in other words, it can transfer a great deal of data every second. It allows you to send information down several channels or 'lines' at the same time. Baseband systems (which only have one channel, such as a normal phone line) are made of twisted copper wire, whereas broadband employs other materials, typically fibre optic cable, to reduce transfer times. Not only can this result in speeds of data transfer that are many times faster than that of modems (meaning a download of an MP3 pop song takes just over a minute, instead of the usual twelve minutes), but the connection is always on, meaning you don't have to connect each time you want to go online – you simply open your browser or e-mail program and away you go. Because it is 'multi-channelled', you can also use the phone, or several phones, and a fax machine at the same time. There are different types of broadband connection, but they all work on this 'multi-channel' principle. The most common for home computer use are ADSL (Asymmetrical Digital Subscriber Line), which actually uses (copper) phone lines, and cable modem.

Where can I get it and how much does it cost?

Considering that broadband was planned to reach most UK households by the end of the 1980s, it's taken its time getting here. But the dawn of the 21st century has finally brought affordable broadband connections to many people; the US is a pioneer in broadband, but the UK is catching it up. The three main providers in the UK are BT (who offer ADSL) and Telewest and NTL, both with cable modem access. While BT fights for its share of the market, the latter two have effectively divided up the territory and are trying to reach the whole of the UK between them. The result is that in many parts of the UK, you can now get fixed-price, broadband Internet use for a very reasonable £25/month, plus a one-off installation fee of £50. Not bad when just a year or so ago, experts were saying it was unlikely to fall below £40/month for the foreseeable future. Find out more about the Telewest and NTL service at www.broadband-cable.co.uk, or by phoning 0800 519 4000. Discover ADSL at the BT website (www.bt.com). Broadband is revolutionary, and is the ultimate way to speed up your surfing.

Tips and tricks for faster surfing – the good old-fashioned way

While you're waiting for broadband to reach your area, or if you don't want to take the plunge just yet, here are some handy ways to gain a few more miles per hour on the information superhighway:

1. **Avoid the rush hour.** Just like our road networks, the information superhighway suffers traffic jams at busy times. When you can, use the Net late at night and early in the morning. Try to avoid late afternoons, evenings, weekends and public holidays.

2. **Personalize your home page.** You can choose your favourite website as your browser's home page, so that page always appears when you log on to the Web. In Internet Explorer, go to the website, then in the Tools menu, choose Internet Options. Click the Use Current and click OK. In Netscape Navigator, open the website, go to the Edit menu and choose Preferences. Click on Navigator, choose Home Page and click Use Current Page.

3. **Tailor sites to your needs.** Portals like Yahoo!

and Excite allow you to customize the information you receive. It's like making a web page, displaying your choice of news, sports, weather and so on.

4. **Find it with Favorites.** Rather than spending ages hunting for that site you found last time, go to the Favorites menu (called Bookmarks in Navigator) and click Add to Favorites. Next time you want to visit the site, simply click on the web address in the Favorites list and you'll go straight there. You can also organize your favourites into folders if you wish, when you go offline.

5. **Open another window.** Don't bother clicking back and forth between web pages – simply open another window in your browser and view the next page there instead – it's quicker. You can also surf two websites at the same time this way, side by side.

6. **Get to know your toolbar.** Getting familiar with your browser's tools can save a lot of time, and make you a more confident surfer. Explorer lets you customize your toolbar, too. Go to the View menu, choose Toolbars, then Customize, and simply add or remove buttons to the toolbar, to suit your needs.

7. **Remember to right-click.** The right-hand mouse button gives you handy pop-up menus that can help you perform the task in hand quickly.

8. **Turn off the animation.** If you just want text, you can browse the Web a lot faster if you turn off the animations and adverts that appear on websites. In Explorer, open the Tools menu and select Internet Options. Click the Advanced tab, and untick the box next to Show Pictures, in the multimedia section. If you do want to view a picture at any time, simply right-click on the empty box where the picture would be, and choose Show Picture (Show Image in Navigator) from the pop-up menu.

9. **Use a download accelerator.** These programs speed up download times by configuring your PC's operating system in the most efficient way. This can result in increasing your download speeds by up to 300 per cent. Try RealDownload (www.real.com), Download Accelerator Plus (www.downloadaccelerator.com) and Surf Express (www.connectix.com).

10. **Zip it up.** Compressing files with WinZip (or Windows Me's built-in 'Compressed Folders' utili-

ty) can reduce file sizes by up to 60 per cent. Send zipped e-mail attachments, and always choose to download a file in a zipped format if you have a choice – it can save a lot of time.

11. **Use search engines effectively.** See 'The Wonder of The World Wide Web' for more detail on this. You can also have a guess at a website by entering www.companyname.com. in the address bar – you never know your luck.

12. **Read the error messages.** The most common error message is '404 – Not Found', meaning your browser can't find the site. This could be a mistype on your part, or it may mean that the page does not exist any more, or has moved. Play around with the web address (for example, remove all the address after the first slash or try .co.uk or .html at the end) to see if you uncover anything. If you get a 'Host unknown' message, this means either that you've lost your connection, or that the server hosting that site is down, probably for maintenance, or that the new URL you've made up is total garbage!

13. **Check for browser updates.** Browsers are updated every now and then, to take account of new technology or to repair bugs. To benefit from these improvements, visit the Internet Explorer site (www.microsoft.com/windows/ie). In Netscape Navigator, go to the Help menu and select Software Updates.

14. **Use keyboard shortcuts.** Navigating with a mouse all the time can be tedious (although the scroll wheel featured on many mice does speed things up a lot). You can use keyboard shortcuts to get there instead. For example:

Up arrow – move up one to two lines

Down arrow – move down one to two lines

Page Up – scroll up one screen

Page Down – scroll down one screen

Home (Ctrl + Home in both Navigator and Internet Explorer) – move to the start of a web page

End (Ctrl + End in Navigator) – move to the end of a web page

Ctrl + N – open a new window in your browser

15. Use the Refresh and Stop buttons. If a page is taking ages to load, reload the page from the start (using the Refresh button on your toolbar) – it could be that you've just hit a glitch with that particular download and it'll be fine next time round. But if it obviously isn't working, click on Stop, go on to another site, and try again later.

16. And finally – take a break! Surfing all day long is no good for your brain or your body. You become less efficient the longer you work without a break, and can suffer severe aches and pains. So remember to take regular breaks from the Web (and from your computer in general) of at least ten minutes every hour – that way, you'll have a much more enjoyable, and efficient, online experience.

GLOSSARY

Active X – A set of controls that helps a program access interactive content on a web page. Because they have access to your operating system, they start working as soon as they are downloaded, without having to be installed first. (NB: ActiveX only works in Internet Explorer.)

address book – The section of your e-mail program where you store the details of your contacts.

ADSL – Asymmetrical Digital Subscriber Line – a type of broadband Internet connection. Asymmetrical means that data can be downloaded faster than it can be uploaded.

analogue – Data sent in continually varying quantities, such as a standard telephone signal. The opposite of digital.

applets – Mini-programs written in the Java programming language that help your browser access certain Web content.

application – Another word for a program, such as Word or Excel.

ARPANET – Advanced Research Projects Agency Network. A system of interlinked computers developed by the US Defense Agency in the Cold War, and the forerunner of the Internet.

attachment – Any file sent with an e-mail that is not part of the e-mail message itself, such as a digital photo or soundclip.

avatar – A character that represents you online in a virtual reality scenario.

AVI – A Microsoft file format for audio-video files.

bandwidth – The amount of data that is transferred in a set amount of time, measured in Kilobits per second (Kbps). A 56K modem therefore has twice the bandwidth of a 28K model.

baseband – A non-broadband Internet connection, such as a telephone line, that can only use one channel at a time to transfer data.

BBS – Bulletin Board System. A pre-Internet computer system allowing access via modem and phone line. Some updated to allow access via Internet as well.

bit – A single unit of digital data.

bookmark – A web address stored by your browser so you can return to it easily. Called a Favorite in Internet Explorer.

broadband – A high-speed Internet connection that can use more than one channel at a time to transfer data and hence transfer more data in a given period.

browser – A program, such as Internet Explorer or Netscape Navigator, that allows you to view web pages.

byte – 8 bits of digital data.

cable modem – A modem used with a high-speed cable Internet connection.

cache – Your browser's temporary store of web pages, which allows you to view them quickly. As the cache fills up, the oldest addresses are deleted to make room.

CERT – Computer Emergency Response Team. A group of computer experts set up to deal with viruses and other computer security issues.

channel – A continual connection to a website, providing constantly updated content to your desktop.

chatroom – A popular group discussion forum that operates in real time.

client – A computer that requests information from a server. The client software (such as a browser) then displays this information. The whole of the Internet runs on this client–server relationship.

cookie – A small text file sent from a website to your hard disk containing information about your visit.

CSNET – Computer Science Research Network. The computer network set up by the scientific community in the 1970s to enable users to exchange research findings easily.

digital – Data sent in the form of ones and zeros, in a constant quantity. The opposite of analogue.

directory – An online database of websites, organized into categories.

domain name – The unique part of an e-mail or website address, after the @ or www., usually indicating the name of the company or server concerned.

download – To transfer data from the Internet to your computer. The opposite of upload.

e-commerce – Electronic commerce. The collective term for any business conducted on the Internet.

e-mail – Electronic mail.

emoticon – A character or symbol used to display emotion in an e-mail message.

encryption – A system of encoding confidential information, often when sending it across the Net, by scrambling the bits of data that it consists of.

FAQ – Frequently Asked Questions. The section of a website or group discussion area where you can read the most common queries that it receives. This prevents the site having to answer the same question over and over again.

favorite – See bookmark.

flaming – Using abusive or provocative language in an e-mail or group discussion, often during an argument with another participant. Considered very poor Netiquette.

Flash – A popular program for creating animation on websites.

freeware – Software that you can download and keep free of charge.

FTP – File Transfer Protocol. The most popular method of transferring files across the Internet.

GIF – Graphics Interchange Format. A graphics file format, developed by CompuServe, used for still and animated images. Gradually being replaced by the PNG (Portable Network Graphics) format.

History – A list displayed by your browser of web pages you have previously visited.

home page – 1. The first or 'cover' page of a website. 2. The web page you see first each time you connect to the Web.

host – A device connected to a computer network, most commonly used to mean a server.

HTML – Hypertext Markup Language. The programming language used for formatting website content.

HTTP – Hypertext Transfer Protocol. The standard way of sending web content across the Net.

HTTPS – Hypertext Transfer Protocol Secure. The secure version of HTTP, used for sending confidential information. A web page address beginning with HTTPS means it is secure.

hyperlink – An icon or text on a website which, when clicked on, will take you to a related page or site. The mouse pointer usually changes to a pointing hand when you pass it over a hyperlink.

IAP – Internet Access Provider. A company that provides only access to the Internet, without additional content or services. Mostly superseded by ISPs.

IMAP – Internet Message Access Protocol. A system for retrieving your incoming mail from your ISP's server. Looks set to replace the more basic POP3 in this role.

Internet – Short for interconnected networks. The global network of computers that allows the Web, e-mail, Usenet and file transfer systems to operate.

Internet Explorer – Microsoft's web browser, which comes as standard with most new computers, or is available free from various sites on the Web.

IP address – The unique address of each PC connected to the Internet. This is a number, and enables each computer to find its intended recipient across the Net.

IRC – Internet Relay Chat. A program that allows participants to chat to each other online in real time.

ISP – Internet Service Provider. A company providing access to, and additional services on, the Internet.

JavaScript – A programming language used to create interactive content on the Web.

JPEG – Joint Photographic Experts Group. A graphics file format, popular for images used on the Web.

KB – Kilobyte. 1024 bytes of digital data.

Kbps – Kilobits per second. A measure of how fast digital data can be sent down a phone line and therefore also a measure of your modem's speed.

link – Short for hyperlink.

lurking – Observing any kind of group interaction on the Web, such as a chatroom, without taking part, for example, in order to understand it better before joining in yourself.

Media player – A plug-in that can play multimedia formats such as audio and video files. RealPlayer is a popular choice.

message board – An online group discussion facility allowing participants to 'post' messages to a virtual noticeboard. Replies appear on the board too, allowing a time-delayed discussion to occur.

metacrawler – A powerful search engine that can search a group of other search engines simultaneously.

MHz – Megahertz. A measurement of the speed of your

PC's processor; 1MHz equals 1 million calculations per second.

modem – Short for modulator/demodulator. The device that converts digital data into analogue, and vice versa, to send and receive it down a telephone line.

MPEG – Moving Pictures Expert Group. A highly compressed video format, developed from the JPEG format.

MUD – Multi-User Dungeon. A system for playing online games, usually with several players.

Netiquette – Short for Net etiquette. A code of conduct for communicating on the Internet.

Netscape Navigator – A popular web browser, its main rival being Microsoft's Internet Explorer.

newsgroups – Discussion areas on the Net, categorized by subject.

newsreader – The software required to view newsgroups. Many browsers have one as standard.

news server – A powerful computer that provides you with access to newsgroups on the Internet.

Outlook Express – Microsoft's popular e-mail

program, which comes as standard with most new PCs.

packet switching – A way of splitting up data into more manageable chunks or 'packets' to send over the Net.

plug-in – Additional software to add on to existing software to give it more functions. RealPlayer is a plug-in for your web browser.

POP3 – Post Office Protocol 3. One of two main systems, along with IMAP, for retrieving incoming e-mail from a server.

program – Software that allows you to interact with your PC to perform a specific task. Word is a program that allows you to perform word processing tasks.

protocol – A 'language' that allows PCs to talk to each other across a network.

proxy server – A secondary server that places itself between a PC and the original server, often to keep the user's details confidential.

QuickTime – Apple's media player.

RealPlayer – A popular media player, from the Real network.

real time – Actions that happen on the Net as if they were happening in real life, i.e. instantaneously. Chatrooms work in this way.

search engine – A database-driven website that can search other sites for information.

server – A powerful computer that handles requests from other computers.

shareware – Software that you can try before you buy.

Shockwave – A popular program for creating animation on the Web.

SMTP – Simple Mail Transfer Protocol. A standard used by servers to allow you to send e-mail.

Spam – Junk e-mail.

spider – Another word for metacrawler.

streaming video/audio – Data sent in a continuous flow or stream, for smooth, uninterrupted viewing.

subscribing – Signing up for a service on the Net, such as a newsletter sent by e-mail.

TCP/IP – Transmission Control Protocol/Internet Protocol. The standard way of moving data across the Net. IP is the unique numerical address of each connected computer. TCP is a quality control system that checks the data transfer for errors, and ensures it arrives in the right order and is delivered to the right program.

ticker – A stream of information delivered to your screen from a website, having the appearance of tickertape.

upload – To send something from your PC to the Internet. The opposite of download.

URL – Uniform (or Universal) Resource Locator. The official term for an address accessed via the Net, such as that of a website or newsgroup.

Usenet – The part of the Internet hosting newsgroups.

V.90 modem – The standard format for today's 56K modems, ensuring they are compatible with modern PCs and the Net.

virtual reality – An artificially created scenario or 'world'.

WAP – Wireless Application Protocol. A stripped-down version of the Web for mobile phones. Rumoured to be replaced by G3 (3rd Generation) phones.

web browser – See browser.

webcam – Web camera. A small camera that can send and receive live images to the Web.

Windows Me – Microsoft's popular operating system, containing Windows Media Player.

WinZip – A program for compressing files, to make them faster to transfer across the Net.

WWW – Abbreviation of World Wide Web, quite often just called 'the Web'.

Yahoo! – The most visited website on the Internet. Packed with interesting features, including web-based e-mail.

Yahooligans – The kids' version of Yahoo!

Zip disk – A storage disk that can hold up to 250MB of data. Requires a Zip drive to use it.

zip files – A compressed file format, shown by the suffix '.zip'. Not related to Zip disks.